IT'S JUST A THOUGHT

Tame Your Mind, Free Your Spirit

John Daughety

Paperback ISBN: 979-8-9855888-0-4
Hard Cover ISBN: 979-8-9855888-2-8
Digital eBook ISBN: 979-8-9855888-1-1

To my husband, David.

Acknowledgments

It would have been impossible to bring this book into the world without the help and encourage-ment of others. Madeleine Calvi's editorial assessment and advice helped me breathe new life into my work. I am exceptionally grateful for the masterful work of my editor Robin Fuller. Her ability to bring clarity and definition to my thoughts while maintaining my voice is awe inspiring. My mother, Kella Boatner, gave the first drafts the benefit of her teacher's eyes. Most of all, I am grateful to my wonderful husband, David, for his encouragement and acting as my sounding board throughout the creation of this book.

There, too, are the countless people I've encountered along my life's journey. Each person, in some way, has added to and helped shape the person I am today. In some way, all have contributed to the ideas and philosophies written on these pages.

Contents

Part One

Chapter One: *A Journey of a Thousand Miles Begins with One Step*

Chapter Two: *It's Just a Thought*

Chapter Three: *The Illusion*

Chapter Four: *Self*

Chapter Five: *Faith*

Chapter Six: *Spirituality*

Chapter Twelve: Forgiveness

Part Three

Chapter Thirteen: *Escaping Hell*

Chapter Fourteen: Into Practice

Chapter Fifteen: Enlightenment

Chapter Sixteen: We Are Gods

Chapter Seventeen: Life After Death

Bibliography

Introduction

"To the mind that is still, the whole universe surrenders."
— Lao Tzu

Our minds are full of thoughts constantly flying in and out of focus, crashing into and often contradicting each other. *It's Just a Thought* shows how and why this happens and how to tame those thoughts, quiet the mind, and free up that energy in order to use it constructively.

When our minds are quiet, we have greater potential to discover and tap into the power of unconditional love that we were born with but didn't realize we had. We become free of the opinions of others and the need to convince other people of who we are. We are free to be authentic and allow others to tell their stories however they want without judging them or being dependent upon their judgment—allowing us to experience true joy and radiate unconditional love.

It's Just a Thought is about realizing your spiritual awakening or even finding your path to enlightenment through the practice of unconditional love. Many obstacles make embodying unconditional love difficult or seemingly impossible. This book will identify and define those obstacles and show you ways to overcome them.

A primary aim of this book is to show you what you

already have and help you appreciate it by removing the illusion of lack or of wanting to be something or someone else. This book isn't meant to change who you are. It's intended to help you see who you truly are already, without the lenses, shades, and distortions of judgment, and the comparisons that leave us feeling like we are "less than."

The method I've used to find my inner peace and spiritual enlightenment comes first through the practice of unconditional self-love. But to find that, you must first understand what unconditional love is and how it feels. Next comes forgiveness. Forgiveness is a direct result of the unconditional nature of love. You need to forgive yourself and give yourself room to grow without judgment or expectations of how your growth should look. When you have removed judgment and resentment from how you perceive yourself, you can then expand that *Love* outside of yourself and love others unconditionally, without judgment, and without expectations of how they ought to be.

Part of our inner peace comes when we have freed ourselves from our self-judgment and the judgment of others. We become immune to criticism and praise because our ego has been pushed to its proper place and we are no longer ruled by it. As we love without conditions or expectations, we are free to accept others just as they are instead of wanting to change them into how we hope they might be. We become authentic, and we can see the authenticity in others—even when they cannot.

You are you, and by your very nature, you are perfect. That's all you've ever needed to be. If you want to change who you are because you think that will make you feel better, you've got a long, challenging, and disappointing road ahead. But when you see who you are, you will feel better because you will be able to love and accept yourself for the perfect, amazing human being that you are and always have been.

I'm not going to make any grand promises about what this book will do for you or how long it will take you to reach your spiritual goals. Everyone is different, and we all start at different stages and places in our lives. Therefore, I encourage you to be patient with yourself. Release your expectations and judgments of where you think you ought to be on your path. I have yet to find an express lane to spiritual awareness. It comes when it comes, and as the Big Book of Alcoholics Anonymous says about its promises of recovery and spiritual and personal growth, "sometimes quickly, sometimes slowly. They will always materialize if we work for them."

Part One

Chapter One: *A Journey of a Thousand Miles Begins with One Step*

"You are a child of the universe no less than the trees and the stars; you have a right to be here."
— *"Desiderata," Max Ehrmann*

You are a Child of the Universe No Less than the Trees

When I started on my journey in earnest, all I wanted was peace. I tried to quiet my mind and silence the jumble of thoughts bouncing around in my head. I wanted an end to the pain I felt, and I wanted to stop hurting myself and others. The knowledge that you and I are meant for something extraordinary and beautiful was innate—but I had no idea how to get there. My journey began with nothing more than *willingness* and a little bit of courage to push beyond the barrier of *Fear* in my mind.

This book isn't about me, but it comes from within me, and there is a lot of me in this book. This book isn't about my experiences, but about what I learned from them and how I think that can help you, too. It might be helpful for you to know a little more about me and how I came to discover this amazing spiritual way.

Like most people, I was born into the religion of my parents. They were both Christians—specifically, Southern Baptists. I knew I wanted to be a preacher by the time I was four years old, even though I didn't understand anything about religion, God, Jesus, doctrine, or dogma. I didn't know about heaven or hell. I didn't know about sin or salvation. All I did know was that I needed to be behind that pulpit, underneath the spotlight, with all eyes focused on me.

My childhood was far from ideal, and it wasn't very nice at times. While I no longer blame or resent anyone who harmed me, that wasn't the case for almost the first half of my life. By the time I was ten years old, I was full of bitterness, anger, and hatred. I had no idea why I was so angry, but I was. I wanted to be a good boy, but I didn't feel like one—so I often wasn't.

One of the side effects of miscommunicated Christian doctrine that I experienced was that I believed that good people received good things and bad people got bad things. That idea had been imprinted in my mind as far back as I can remember. I had a lot of terrible things happen to me before my age even reached double digits, so in my little mind, I was logically a horrible person.

When I was about six years old, something awful was happening. I don't remember exactly what was going on at the time; maybe it was my paternal grandmother's death. But I remember being alone in a room, and I thought I should pray. Instead of praying, I just said, "Dear God, I hate you." I didn't want to hate God, but for whatever reason, my six-year-old self wasn't too pleased with Him.

That was the beginning of a love-hate relationship with the God I had inherited. As time passed, in the care of my divorced mother, my behavior grew worse and worse. The concerted judgment of my elders was that I was just a spoiled brat. I was entitled and prone to monstrous tantrums; I broke things for no apparent reason; I pouted a lot; I was rude. Not all the time, mind you, but enough to earn the title of "spoiled brat." I think, though, that if the adults had had the slightest idea of what was actually going on with me, their judgment would have been different. But they did the best they could with the information they had available to them.

I'm sure you can guess that my adolescence was even worse. I ran with the "bad" kids—smoked, drank, and used drugs. But even then, I tried to have a relationship with the God I had inherited. I'd swing back into church and kick up a whirlwind of zeal, only to burn out and drift away again. And when I drifted away, it was often into depression and destructive behavior.

By the time I reached seventeen years of age, I had learned how to stay relatively calm for extended periods of time. I even swung back into church and decided that I was "called" to the ministry. That feeling hasn't gone away, but it was no longer about the attention at that age. I thought it was about my love of God and how I wanted to share that with everyone else. I still have that "share it with everyone else" mentality to this day—just not in the same way. But like so many times before, that zeal faded, and I faded away with it.

Three years later, that zeal returned, but much stronger than before. This time, I followed through and went to college to study for the ministry. I earned a ministerial scholarship and moved a couple of states away, attending a Southern Baptist college with a major in religion and a minor in psychology. If you're noticing the pattern, it was still in force: after a couple of years, I felt myself pulling away from my religion—not for lack of zeal, but due to something much different and more profound.

In retrospect, the pattern I described is perfectly understandable. I wanted to feel the closeness to God that I saw in others. I wanted to be as high on Jesus as they were. But I believed that bad things happened to bad people, and therefore, I must be bad. I didn't have a clue as to what I could have done so wrong to have earned such torment, but I couldn't help but believe the failure was my own. In defense of the Bible, and to be fair, I should recall a verse from the Gospel of Matthew: "For he makes his sun to rise on the evil and the good, and sends rain on the just and the unjust" (Matthew 5:45). I like to think that this was Jesus's way of saying, "Stuff happens; don't take it personally."

I did, however, take it personally. And I also figured out what was "wrong" with me that must have made God hate me: I'm gay. Although I hadn't yet acted on my sexuality, I had the thoughts in my mind, and since God knew my thoughts, I knew I couldn't hide from Him. I tried to be the way I thought God wanted me to be. I had girlfriends and eventually married my college sweetheart, but I knew there was nowhere to hide. So, in my junior year, I switched my major and minor and finished school with a degree in psychology.

I had been on track for the ministry and was slated to be licensed as a minister. In my church, licensure was the first step toward ordination and would allow me to preach and get paid for it. I'd have been a substitute preacher within the state conference. Eventually, after I graduated and went to seminary, I'd be ordained and start a full-time vocation in ministry. Instead, I changed my major at school and walked away from a career in ministry.

I am grateful for the way leaving the ministry unfolded, but it was heartbreaking at the time. When I left the ministry, I abandoned my church, too. I realized—or so I thought—that my differences with God were irreconcilable. I believed I was too flawed to be saved unless God miraculously changed me (which all the doctrine and evidence were clearly against). So, I moved on to worship my career and the money it brought me.

There was always a hole in the center of my being that I could never fill. I'd thought that was where God was supposed to go, but it was just an empty place since He didn't want me. Sometimes I felt I could fill it with alcohol, but that didn't work out very well.

Despite my success, I longed for something bigger than money, property, or prestige. My marriage was all right (until it wasn't), and I had more than I needed, yet I was unfulfilled. In my mind, it always came back to something spiritual. I took another try at religion and converted to Roman Catholicism. That lasted a couple years, but it didn't scratch the itch, so again I drifted away.

Then one day, my entire world came crashing down around me. At the time, I was extremely depressed, and I hurt so bad inside that I could feel nothing but pain. I contemplated suicide many times, but I didn't want to die; I just wanted the horrible pain and emptiness to go away. I wanted some relief. Drunk and in a pit of despair, I made decisions that would end in catastrophe. I lost my marriage (which was pretty much over by then anyway), my house, my car, my job, my reputation, and my freedom, all in one day. I was fortunate that I didn't hurt anyone—at least, not physically—because that would likely have changed the path I landed on drastically. And despite the pain, drama, and trauma, today I am deeply grateful for those awful decisions, because they led to something more amazing than I could ever have imagined.

I suppose it's possible that I could have had a spiritual awakening and gained the spiritual insight I have today without all that trauma and drama. But the hardships have shaped the way I communicate and empathize with people. That alone makes it worth it, and I am grateful. I have been able to share what I've learned with people in a way that has allowed them to avoid much of the misery I experienced.

Though I am no longer religious, nor a preacher, I still feel like a minister—but in the archaic meaning of that word: "a person used to convey something." I still have something to proclaim, but it isn't something hard to understand or gain—and it is freely available to anyone, no strings attached.

I will relate more about some of my experiences in the following chapters. Before I do, though, I want to make sure I'm clear about something that I think is very important for anyone seeking spiritual relief.

The most significant cause of my spiritual pain was that I could not change who I truly was—but in truth, I didn't want to. Somewhere in our minds is the knowledge that we are perfect. The problems begin when we deny our nature, deny our perfection, and build masks and walls to protect us from the danger of being seen as "not good enough." Wrongly, we learn that we can only love and accept ourselves if others love and accept us. If others criticize or abuse us, we are likely to criticize and abuse ourselves, too.

We also know, somewhere in our minds, that this isn't fair and it isn't true. But we get stuck in the game that everyone else is playing. The game depends on our externally based self-perception. If we only see ourselves through the eyes of others, we are much easier to manipulate, and likewise, others are easier to manipulate. I don't like that game.

It took something extreme (something that nearly killed me several times over) for me to see myself for who and what I am—my true self. Having an empty and quiet mind was the key that allowed that to happen. I had no one left to impress, and I no longer cared what anyone thought of me. I'd lost everything I thought was important. I was just a shell—but I was a shell that was at least grateful to still be alive. And with my mind quiet and still, I was no longer distracted by the thoughts put into my mind by others. I no longer had a reason to portray myself as the person others expected me to be. I had no reason to be anything other than who or whatever I was in that moment. For the first time since I was six years old, I was authentic—and when I looked in the mirror one day, I truly loved the person I saw staring back at me.

I have had the joy and privilege of being able to relate the things I've learned in the hope that nobody has to go through the extremes that I went through before I could see the truth. I've been fortunate to see the distillation of those experiences helping others to see themselves truthfully, too.

* * *

The most important thing to remember about a spiritual journey is that it is a *journey*. We are meant to enjoy the journey, and if it isn't joyful, there are always new roads to follow. The spiritual journey is lifelong. The longer we're at it, the better it gets.

If you have opened this book, there is a good chance that you are a *Seeker*—someone on a quest for enlightenment, happiness, spiritual fulfillment, and truth. I cannot claim to have all the answers, but I might have some that will resonate with you. Perhaps this is nothing more than a signpost along your journey, or maybe this is the answer you've been looking for all along. I hope that I might share a bit of the flame and light that burns within me—and that flame will add to yours.

I hope that what I share with you will give you a spark of light. This book is about connecting with the God inside you. We can only perceive the universe around us through our thoughts. Therefore, what we *think* shapes everything about us and impacts every facet of our well-being. While *It's Just a Thought* is the title, this book is about much more than that. Our *thought life* is the gateway to inner peace and *Love*.

As we take this journey together, you will notice that I use the word *thought* repeatedly. Everything we do, say, and dream results from a thought. Until we learn to quiet the mind, thoughts rule everything about us. Thoughts create a lot of noise in the mind; many thoughts contradict each other and compete for our attention. Have you ever felt your thoughts racing around in your mind like ice cubes in a blender—thoughts bouncing off of each other so fast and so hard that you can't seem to grasp a single one? Have you ever been concentrating on a task, and some random thought unrelated to anything in that moment in your life pops up in your mind like a shout in an empty room?

The only thing in the universe that can prevent us from connecting to the true *Source of Love* is our thoughts. Our inner voice speaks to us through thoughts. It often speaks to us as if the voice is coming from another person, but it is still us—our ego. If we give ourselves over to the *Source of Love,* we will be less and less chained to the thoughts in our minds. As a result, kindness and gentleness will flow through and from us naturally.

Living in a state of grace, peace, joy, and bliss, and just being present in the moment—in the now—is the natural state of all things, including you. We are not born into this world to suffer. We are born to experience the wonder of the universe and join with it as one. We are meant to tap into the *Source* and let its *Love* flow through us. The closer we become with the *Source*—with *Love*—the greater our sense of peace, harmony, and love. The more that *Love* radiates from us, the greater our impact on the world around us. Taken a step further, the more of us who join in *Love*, the closer we all are to realizing heaven on earth.

* * *

Throughout this book, I use certain words that may have multiple meanings. In most cases, when I use a word as a specific term, I will emphasize it with *italics* and/or *Capitalize* it. The most common words I use in this way are *Love*, the *Source*, and *Fear*.

The word *Source* refers to the force or energy responsible for all creation. *Love* is the *Source*, and the *Source* is *Love*. I use the words *Love* and *Fear* because we are familiar with the feelings, emotions, and ideas these words evoke within us. They are energetic forces that connect and flow through everything. *Love* is the will, intent, and pure essence of the *Source*. *Fear* describes the absence of *Love*. Paradoxically, *Fear* does not exist, but we can feel its emptiness mentally, emotionally, and physically. Another way to think of *Fear* is to compare it to cold. In physics, cold doesn't exist. Cold is just a word to describe the absence of heat, but we can feel that absence, and we call it cold. Likewise, when the energy and power of *Love* are blocked, we feel that lack in some manifestation and form of *Fear*.

It is essential to understand that these terms are not the same as the emotions we call love and fear. *Love* can evoke those warm, fuzzy, euphoric feelings we often call love, and *Fear* can manifest as being afraid, nervous, or worried. But *Fear* is much more than that. The absence of *Love* can also manifest as anger, resentment, guilt, and regret. *Fear* causes us to build obstacles that prevent us from realizing *Love* and allowing it to flow through and radiate from us—like ice building up, preventing heat from reaching whatever is encased by the ice.

I also use the word *God*. I use this word interchangeably with *Love*, and I use it to capture the essence of the connection that all spirits—our spirits—have with the *Source*. In his book *The Power of Now*, Eckhart Tolle says that the word *God* is empty and without meaning because of persistent misuse. And when I use the word *God*, I do not mean a person or personality. I simply mean the *Source—Love—*and a connection to it that is so profound and beautiful that it embodies the qualities of the divine.

* * *

This book can help us break the cycles that keep us locked in a cage of *Fear*, preventing us from realizing our rightful place as manifestations of *Love* itself. Wherever you are on your journey, I am hopeful that there is something of value for you in these pages. It's up to you how far you will go along your chosen path and the paths yet to be revealed.

Early on in my journey, I wanted to feel at peace and be able to love myself. As I studied the writings and teachings of various spiritual leaders and religious and spiritual texts, I wanted a deeper connection with *Love*. Enlightenment seemed interesting, but I was happy to at least be awake. I wasn't quite sure what being "enlightened" meant anyway. I thought it was something a bit out of reach.

I was mistaken. As I now know and understand it, enlightenment is as simple as having spiritual wisdom and maturity. It only takes willingness and practice to achieve it. To live in a state of enlightened grace is your birthright. It is your natural state. I will show you how—or at least point you in a good direction—to achieve this state of being.

There is another state of being beyond enlightenment, and that is transcendence. There are many schools of thought on this subject, and an abundance of fascinating reading. Some say you must meditate deeply and continually to achieve transcendence. Some say you can achieve it through the indwelling of the Holy Spirit by accepting Christ "as your Lord and savior." However, I believe that transcendence is more of a psychological construct. It comes when we quiet the noise of so many thoughts and allow ourselves to listen to the silence of a mind at peace.

I think many possibilities and many paths lead to the same destination. None is better than the other, and I have yet to find anything remotely resembling a universal technique. The one common element is *Love*; beyond that, to each their own. I found transcendence along the way. I wasn't looking or striving for it, but I found peace and an enlightened understanding of *Love*.

I remember where I was, but I don't quite remember what I was doing—paperwork of some sort, some repetitive task that allowed me to clear my mind and enter a meditative state while I did it. As I sat there doing my work, oblivious to the world around me, I suddenly felt a flood of knowledge. It wasn't knowledge that came from learning or experience; it was *all* knowledge. In an instant, I knew how this and every other universe works. I knew why the universe works the way it does. I knew why we are all here. I knew the beginning and the end of all time.

I was also acutely aware that the knowledge was not mine. It was as if I were plugged into a vast storehouse of wisdom and could access whatever I wanted. I didn't have to know what I wanted to know; it was like *Knowledge* itself anticipated what I wanted to know. I was just utterly ecstatic that I'd somehow tapped into it.

I don't know how long that lasted—a few minutes, or a few hours—but as I got back to the rest of my day, that knowledge slowly slipped out of my grasp. I remembered that I knew something amazing, but I had no way to tell what it was. Reflection and research helped me understand that this knowledge has always been there, but the noise of my many thoughts prevented conscious access to it. I will go into this in more detail in Chapter 15, but this phenomenon is what Carl Jung called the *collective unconscious.*

The experience of such *Knowledge* has happened to me several times since then. Sometimes it would happen when I was doing some simple task, meditating, or having a conversation with someone to whom I was giving spiritual guidance. The common element was that I was "plugged into" the *Source.* I was either in contemplation or meditation, or talking about eternal *Love.*

There are three things I want to say about this experience. First, it is the most fantastic feeling of bliss I have ever encountered. Second, to step away from that state is painless and without regret. Third, I don't want to stay there all the time. This may be surprising since, as I said, it is the most powerful and incredible sensation of peace and joy; however, there must always be balance in the universe and ourselves.

There are things that I enjoy in this playground of life, and those things demand attention and care. There are people I like to help and work with who probably couldn't relate to me while I'm in that state. To be fully transcendent is a solitary pursuit, and for whatever is gained, something is lost. There *must* be balance.

* * *

We have so many thoughts in our minds at any given moment that it is hard to filter out the chatter from what is important. We have thoughts meant to help us achieve a goal, but we also have other thoughts driven by our fear and our egos that crash, collide, contradict, and distract us from where our focus should be. Quieting our minds and taming our thoughts will help us find our spiritual center and benefit us by enhancing our focus on the things we are trying to do.

Throughout this book, a common thread runs from beginning to end: quiet your mind and tame your thoughts. We need a basic understanding of what that means. Let's try a little exercise to get a sense of how that quiet might feel. For this exercise, you will benefit most from a quiet space free from distractions. Turn off or silence your electronic devices. This exercise is quite simple, and you can do this any time you need to regain your focus, even for just a little while.

Look around you and notice the first object that comes to your attention. We want to focus on something about the object rather than the object itself. What color is it? What shape is it? Is it tall or short, narrow or wide? The best adjective for this exercise is a single syllable, but that isn't required. We're just after something simple.

Look at the object, and think of the adjective you chose. Right now, I'm looking at a large blue cup. The word I've chosen is *blue*. I didn't select *cup*, because that is the general name of the object. I could have selected *tall*, *large*, or even *round*. But I chose *blue* because that was the first adjective that came to mind.

Carefully look at the object and repeat the adjective silently in your mind for about ten seconds. Close your eyes and envision the object. Then take a deep breath, and as you slowly exhale, whisper the word you selected. I've closed my eyes, and I can see the blue cup in my mind. I've taken a deep breath, and as I exhale, I whisper the word "bluuuuuuuuuuuuue."

Your breathing should be at an average pace. Repeat this breathing and whispering cycle until the only thought in your mind is the word you chose. It is possible that a new thought will barge in that says something like, "Hey! I'm not thinking other thoughts!" Or your attention might slip as you try to inventory any other thoughts that pop up. Don't worry about that. Just repeat the breathing and whispering cycle again.

You can perform this meditation for as long as you like, but three to five minutes should be fine in the beginning. As you practice, you can extend the time that you meditate. But if you find yourself getting bored or frustrated, or your thoughts just won't be quiet, don't worry. Forgive your thoughts for intruding, but do not be frustrated with yourself. Just come back another time and try again. Remind yourself that this is just an exercise and that there is no perfect or imperfect way to do it, and there is no ideal or imperfect result. It is just an exercise.

The goal is to block out any thought other than the word you're using as a mantra. Thoughts will infiltrate your meditation, but there will be gaps when you are breathing where there are no thoughts at all. Notice those gaps. With practice, you'll be able to sustain the silence in your mind for more extended periods.

Even if you have difficulty quieting your mind, practicing this meditation is beneficial. You are telling yourself that you are willing to tame your thoughts, and that willingness is essential. Be proud of taking the time to do something good for yourself.

When you're done, don't forget to turn on and unsilence your electronic devices.

Chapter Two: *It's Just a Thought*

> *"I don't envision a single thing that,*
> *when unguarded, leads to such great harm*
> *as the mind."*
> — *The Buddha*

All Perception Begins as a Thought

Brush, paint, palette, and canvas are merely elements; the thoughts in the artist's mind arrange those elements to create a painting. The final picture is an expression of the artist's thoughts. It is then displayed for anyone to look at it and derive their own thoughts.

Your brain is constantly thinking. Some thoughts are conscious, and some are subconscious. Our subconscious thoughts are the engine that drives the machine. The outside world and our imaginations provide too much information for our conscious mind to process. Our subconscious takes as much of the overflow as it can and stores it in short-term memory, ranks the information by importance (not very accurately), and stores the remainder in long-term memory.

Our brains are incredible machines—powerful, but delicate. Everything the brain does is done with thoughts. Thoughts even control your bodily functions; internal computations constantly evaluate information and stimuli to regulate the body's responses or tell you it's time to run and hide from the lions. While our thoughts may be segregated into conscious and subconscious sections of our minds, our emotions are unfettered and can go wherever they want. Our emotions can easily change or distort our thoughts. Emotions can even have an impact on autonomic and motor functions.

In this way, everything we experience or do is connected to a thought. As I write these words, I'm not only thinking about what I want to say or how I want to say it, I'm thinking about the mass of information I've collected during the lifetime I've lived. I'm thinking about the words I should use to best convey my ideas. I'm thinking about how it will sound in your mind when you read it. As you read, you take in these words and color them with your own experiences, biases, and perspectives; this happens automatically and unconsciously and is unavoidable. That's just how the brain works. The sum of your experiences, emotions, and imagination evaluates the words as you read them. Even before you are finished with a sentence, you've judged the words, formed an opinion, and decided on their meaning—specifically, what they mean to you.

The mind needs to make sense of what it experiences— words on a page, clouds in the sky, dreams, ideas, and imagination. All the senses (some being enhanced when others are not active) feed our minds with a constant flood of information and stimulation. At the same time, the brain is creating its own information and stimuli with memory, imagination, and ideas.

The mind is constantly judging, too. It evaluates anything it receives, as well as all its own thoughts. It judges like a judge in a courtroom. It applies whatever moral and ethical framework you've accepted (your personal law)—whether your conscious mind agrees with those laws or not. You may consciously believe that racial inequity and injustice are wrong, but your internal law may be biased. You may know in your conscious mind and heart that you are a good person, but the judge in your mind accuses and convicts you anyway.

* * *

French philosopher René Descartes famously wrote, "I think; therefore I am." In this perspective, only the mind (or thoughts) are sure to exist, and any knowledge outside of that is uncertain. In a way, this holds true. Whatever we perceive to exist *does* exist in our minds—as thoughts. Input from our senses generates the thoughts that form our perceptions. We see or touch a tree, and our brain converts the sensory impulses into thoughts. If we have prior experience with or knowledge of a tree, our brain compares these new thoughts to our memories. In whatever way our memories are stored, they are always experienced as thoughts when accessed. So then, when we have another experience with a tree—the same one or another—our mind processes the experience into thoughts.

Thought also dominates the ways we receive information. Think about a recent conversation you've had. How are you taking in the information when someone is speaking to you? Your brain translates the sound that reaches your ears into words and images. It's the same with reading. Your brain translates the symbols of the letters that you see—or feel, if reading Braille—into words, images, and ideas. These are nothing but thoughts.

This is an important idea. When we consider what we're after and what might be holding us back (for example, "My goal is enlightenment, but my resentments are in the way"), we can see that everything is happening in our minds. It isn't our circumstances that bring us joy or sorrow; it's only how we feel about them. Suppose I tell someone a story of something tragic that happened to me as a child. They might say, "Oh, that's so terrible. I'm so sorry that happened to you." But why? To me, whatever happened is just a thing that happened. It may be something that hurt me and caused long-lasting pain or dysfunction, but that experience guided my footsteps in some way. Those footsteps led me to where I am today. I cannot know what would have happened otherwise or what I would be like had that thing not occurred.

With all this talk about thoughts and how they manipulate our perceptions, it is critically important to understand that perception is ultimately false. It isn't real— not by a long shot. This is a bit more of a philosophical and psychological concept. Still, the truth is that even though we may think we know something, it has been colored and reshaped within our minds by thoughts that are usually unreliable.

Our biases are some of the strongest subconscious thoughts we have. Those biases change our perception of certain things instantly. Suppose I don't like the color red. Everything I see that is colored red becomes *less than* in my mind. Someone I love may give me a red sweater as a gift, but because of my bias against that color, my thoughts will diminish the value of and my appreciation for that gift.

I might even forget that it is the gesture of giving that is important, rather than the gift itself. On the other hand, if my favorite color is yellow, and my friend gives me a yellow sweater, how much more will I think of the gift? I may even be so delighted with the sweater that I forget to appreciate the gesture of the giving.

A near infinite number of examples can be offered to illustrate this simple truth: perception is not reality. This wasn't an easy idea for me to accept. The ache in my back feels real. The chair I'm sitting on feels real. The touch of someone's hand on my shoulder feels real. But that's not the same as my perception of those things. The objects and actions are real indeed, but what happens inside my mind after perceiving those things becomes altered instantly and unconsciously. When I started seeing how my thoughts and biases reshaped my perceptions, I understood how my perceptions were disconnected from reality.

So, what is real? What *is real* is that you exist. You know you exist because you are aware. The only other thing that truly exists is *Love*. Maybe that's cheating a little, because I know that everything is made from *Love*, so, logically, everything exists! But that only covers what exists; the question remains: what is real? If perception isn't reality, how can we ever tell what's real and what's false?

If that has your head spinning a bit, don't worry; that's just the mind trying to think of a solution. To know what is real, we need to move beyond the basic tools (thoughts) that the mind uses. We need to open up and be available for *Love*'s pure energy to fill every atom of our being. Ironically, this is something that we have to think of first. We need to decide to bring our focus to *this moment right now*.

You Can Change Your Mind

Becoming self-aware is a process that starts at birth. To some degree, all of us are self-aware, as that is the defining characteristic of sentience. Self-awareness can run much deeper, though. When we stop thinking about who we are and instead learn to live in the moment, our awareness shifts away from an arbitrary list of our own qualities to that of oneness with *Love*/God. That is what it means to be mindful. Mindfulness is the ability to be in and aware of the moment, to be present in the now. Being mindful allows you to tune out the noise the world is always buzzing with, and it will silence your inner judge.

Early in my journey, I learned about all these concepts, including mindfulness. I could see the benefits of practicing this, and I wanted them as quickly as possible. I suppose I did "get it" relatively quickly—depending on how you define the word *quick*. Rather than speed, however, I needed practice. I had to break away from the thoughts that caused me to listen to the judge instead of the truth. That took a lot of practice, and I am still practicing and mastering that today. I won't assume that these concepts are equally as challenging for others as they were for me. Some get them right away, and some take years to master them—but if we give it our best honest try, we can all achieve mindfulness and inner peace.

Like so many other *Seekers*, I've pored over many books, videos, lectures, and recordings, trying to find that one trick or technique that would put all the pieces together. It didn't come that easy for me. What I have right now and what I am sharing with you is an amalgam of what I've learned and practiced. My philosophy contains elements of Christianity, Buddhism, Hinduism, Toltec wisdom, New Age thought, and many philosophical and psychological paradigms. I took some elements from each and added them to my own thought life.

I offer just one set of ideas and thoughts, and you are welcome to use them however you like, or discard them wholesale. Nobody can tell you what or how to believe; it's up to you to decide what makes you comfortable and helps you understand yourself, others, and the world around you. This is what it means to be a *Seeker of Truth*.

* * *

All change starts with intention. It is within my will that I start contemplating change. From that intention and willingness, I form the thoughts that lead to actions. Those actions may manifest as studying, meditation, or just stopping some habit that is hurting me.

Remember that we're talking about changing our minds, changing our thoughts, and changing how we react to our thoughts. We aren't trying to change who we are, but to discover (or rediscover) ourselves by removing the debris piled up from years of ego-driven lies. We want to see the image of our true selves and say, "I love you." We want to switch the dependency dynamic so that our ego is dependent on our identity and not the other way around.

The world challenges us constantly and tries to

grab our attention. Natural disasters, political upheaval, crime, and other calamities tug on our sympathy, empathy, and emotions. Random acts of kindness, realized justice, loss restored, or someone accomplishing a dream despite insurmountable odds touch our hearts and build hope. Did you judge any of that as good or evil? I did. I thought, *What can I write that will sound good or evil?* and then wrote those words. That is different from the inner judge, and the discernment of good and evil is somewhat subjective. I'll get into this in more detail later on. Still, I want to address this here while we're talking about changing our minds, or our ways of thinking, including judgments and attitudes that belong to society as a whole rather than our individual tastes and opinions. These things are malleable and often change over time.

In 1952, one of the world's preeminent mathematicians and scientists, Alan Turing, and his same-sex lover were convicted in England of "gross indecency." Given a choice between prison and probation, Turing chose probation. Part of that agreement was that he would submit to hormone treatments to stifle his libido. This treatment has been called "chemical castration." Despite Turing's pivotal accomplishments in cracking the German Enigma code machine in World War II, he was made to suffer under this unnecessary punishment until he finally took his own life.

Any manner of arguments about justice can be made here. But if we look at this through our modern lens, we will probably not see much justice in it at all. Besides the tragedy of Alan Turing's fatal despair, we have a massive shift in the judgment meted out by society. If Turing were thirty-nine years old today, he would be free to have a relationship with a man or even marry him. So, if we wish, we can judge a system that, by current standards, seems cruel and unfair.

Therein lies the rub. Our own judge lives in our subconscious, constantly evaluating everything we do and are, and often undermining our happiness and peace. Likewise, families, tribes, communities, cities, countries, and the world itself all have a judge made up of everyone's collective judges—often with the loudest ones winning out. It's easy to just go along with whatever judgment rules the day, but it's a trap that will keep our inner judge in power over our lives. The key to being free of that judge is a change in our thinking habits and the adoption of mindfulness.

I hope that this change will happen quickly for anyone undertaking it, but it was pretty tricky for me. So much poison and fear were packed into my heart, mind, and soul that had to be cleaned up before I could begin to realize the power of changing my mind. The habits of my thought life did not go away quickly. There's a line from the film *City Slickers* that I appreciate. The trail guide of a dude ranch retreat, Curly (Jack Palance) says to a guest, Mitch (Billy Crystal), "Y'all come up here about the same time with the same problems. You spend fifty weeks a year getting knots in your rope, and you think two weeks up here will untie them for you." That's a fair assessment of the beginning of my spiritual journey! I'd spent a lifetime getting knots in my rope and adding to the tangle. When I'd finally had enough and became willing to change the way I think, I realized that I had a lot of work ahead of me.

The Big Book of Alcoholics Anonymous has this to

say: "Do not be discouraged. No one among us has been able to maintain anything like perfect adherence to these principles. We are not saints. The point is that we are willing to grow along spiritual lines. The principles we have set down are guides to progress. We claim spiritual progress rather than spiritual perfection."

I was fortunate to have those words from the Big Book in my toolkit early on. It helped me appreciate that my path had everything to do with the journey and little to do with the destination. What was I looking for? I wanted peace and happiness, but in the beginning, I didn't put too much thought into a spiritual awakening or enlightenment. I simply need to do *something*.

There are many methods to get our thinking in order and put an end to the judge. I absorbed several of them and made that my practice. I know that how I feel is entirely up to me, even in the extreme. If I am assaulted or harmed, it's my choice how I will react—emotionally or otherwise. It's up to me to allow my ego to be bruised. I choose to be insulted when I want to. I choose to be outraged by what I decide is injustice. That is the freedom of a change of mind. It's my choice. I'll be pissed off if I want to, and I don't have to judge myself for it. I will feel the effects of *Fear* and ingest the psychic poison. That should be punishment enough! This is taking personal responsibility for my thoughts and feelings and accepting the consequences, whether toxic or nourishing.

* * *

It's up to you what thoughts you create or what to do with thoughts that pop up. It's up to you to define who and what you are with your thoughts. It isn't a job that anyone else can do for us. I will always be getting to know myself, because I am continually growing and changing— even when I'm sitting still. How I think and behave now is different from how I thought and behaved twenty years ago, and from how I will be twenty years from now.

If we can understand and agree that, perceptually, all we are is what we think, then we find that we don't need anybody else's thoughts to define who we are or how we ought to be. I am who I want to be, and I will become who I want to be. It's nice to be around people who like me, because it's fun to commune with others. But it's okay if someone doesn't like me. If I become aware of their dislike, I might try to understand what I have done to offend them, but I'm not going to worry about it or doubt who I am. Some people aren't going to like me, and I'm not going to alter myself to change that. That's just a trick, and it's dishonest. I am who I am. If you like me, that's great! If you don't, that's great, too!

We can only control our own thoughts. We have neither the ability nor the right to try and control the thoughts of others. You may be skilled at influencing the thoughts of others, but it will always be up to each person how that influence manifests. That's not to say that a con artist has an excuse; they are responsible for the way they use the power of their words and abilities, just as we all are.

Without access to any statistics, my best guess is that most humans on this planet are unaware of the power their minds have over them or that they are trapped in a nightmare. People seem to gravitate toward conflict and drama. Social media has exploded with so much anger, fear, and hatred. I know people who seemed so peaceful and calm just a few years ago and are now filled with so much negativity and frustration. I found myself getting caught up emotionally in heated arguments. I also found myself judging everyone as good or bad for their choices, depending on whether I agreed with them or not. Is this normal? No, but it is all too common. However, there is an alternative state of consciousness that does not fill your chest with burning poison.

I have no judgment against myself for slipping backward into the hellscape of human fear and anger. It didn't happen because I didn't know better; it happened because I chose to fill my mind with those thoughts. I decided to think I was being righteous (I was only being judgmental and self-righteous). I could have occupied my thoughts with *Love*, but I gave into the judge instead and let it feast on my fear. When I started feeling bad emotionally, and trivial things began to irritate me, I knew I had to change my mind or continue to suffer. The more the internal judge is fed, the stronger it gets and the harder it is to resist. That is more a matter of habituation than it is anything mystical. You can get used to the drama and the trauma in a way that makes it hard to recognize there is a more comfortable and peaceful way to be.

In the simplest terms, the journey of a thousand miles begins with a single step. The first step—and the only requirement—is the willingness to change. Sometimes that willingness comes from pain. Other times, it may come from a desire to expand one's horizons. Sometimes that willingness may have no reason or catalyst at all. But regardless of cause or circumstance, willingness is just a thought, a choice.

Once we make the decision to change, we begin the work. We have to understand and agree that what we want is *truth*. We need to learn how to quiet the noise in our heads and stop thinking so much. We begin with meditation and practice, getting better and better each time.

We can never really stop thinking; that would be impossible. However, the idea is that we stop believing that what we think is real or true. We need to accept that our perceptions are generally unreliable and that, if left to themselves, it is doubtful that our untamed thoughts will ever bring us inner peace. And if we only have a vague idea of what we're looking for—happiness, peace, enlightenment, transcendence—then our thoughts alone can't possibly provide it. We need to go beyond the limits of what our thoughts can provide and reach out for truth.

Thoughts are tools. We need them to make honest assessments and good decisions. The brain is a computer that solves problems, but it is unaware of and unconcerned with the bigger picture. It only wants information. However, within our mind and body is a spirit—or *soul*, if you like. It doesn't exist to serve the brain, but we can train our brains to serve the spirit. When we do this, we have so much potential to excel and strengthen our connection to the *Source*, because we can then reclaim the massive amounts of energy we spend on maintaining *Fear*.

With willingness and effort, we can transform our thoughts. With transformed thoughts, we can clear away the blockages that prevent *Love* from flowing through us. I used to think that this was easier said than done, but that isn't true. The energy of *Love* that surrounds us is tuned to help us. It is as if it wants us to succeed. It is, in a way, inviting us in.

It is very important to be patient and courageous at the beginning of such a transformation. We must be patient with ourselves and with those around us. After all, we have been habituated to tuning into all the noise in the world and filtering for the bits that satisfy our egos and reinforce our beliefs. The noise is everywhere—on the street, in the news, on social media, in our music, on television, in films, at work, at school, or at home.

Changing mental habits takes time and practice. Just remember that there is no schedule that you have to meet. There is no way to fail—even if you don't try. When you are ready, you will put one foot in front of the other and move toward the *Source*, to *Love*. Anyone who desires to feel and be better has everything they need to reach a state of connectedness with the *Source*, experience the joy of being a conduit for *Love*, and live each day with joy.

⋆ ⋆ ⋆

Do you have or have you had a habit that you thought was bad for you, but you just wouldn't stop? Is there some behavior you feel you'd like to change, but you haven't gotten around to it?

I know I have. I'll skip my drinking problem, because that worked itself out dramatically, and the will to not drink has been firm ever since. So, I'll talk about my smoking. I smoked cigarettes for at least thirty years. I knew it was bad for me from the very beginning. When I was in junior high school, I was a runner. I loved to run long distances and cross-country. After I started smoking cigarettes, I couldn't run as fast or as long as I used to, so I quit running. In the end, I liked smoking more.

As I got older, of course, my doctors all told me to stop smoking and would tell me all the horrible things I was doing to my body and the terrible end I was creating for myself. It didn't scare me, and it didn't motivate me to stop smoking. I liked smoking cigarettes. I knew I needed to quit smoking, but I didn't truly want to. But finally, I smelled someone who smoked more than I did, in enclosed spaces. I realized that, to everyone else, I probably smelled just as bad as that person did to me.

It wasn't about what people thought of me smelling bad. By that point, I was already past needing anyone else's approval to define who I am or make me happy. But the smell informed me that there was much less to like about smoking than there was to dislike. It was, I suppose, a cumulative effect, where all the reasons to quit finally outweighed the only reason not to: that I liked smoking cigarettes. So, I changed my mind, and I quit smoking.

The same thing works for thoughts that we are addicted to. We become addicted to the approval of others. We become addicted to comparing ourselves to what we perceive as ideals. We become addicted to drama and conflict. These thoughts assail and harm us, but we aren't willing to let them go because we like something about them. The question, then, is "What is going to tip the balance?"

If I'm addicted to having people praise me and tell me how wonderful I am, I will get a rush from that. But what happens if someone criticizes me instead? What if I believe they might be telling the truth? No matter how slight or severe, there will be damage to my ego. Of course, I could recharge by doing something that usually gets people to praise me and then move on, but this is a cycle. Eventually, I will get my feelings hurt again, and all that good stuff that I crave will be overshadowed by the stink of that one insult.

It helps if we can identify these patterns so that we can see them for what they are and what effect they have on our minds. We'll look at those together, and then we'll see what we can do to change our minds from dependent to independent.

Chapter Three: *The Illusion*

*"Reality is merely an illusion, albeit a
very persistent one."*
— Albert Einstein

Why the World We Perceive is an Illusion

So many spiritual teachers and philosophers refer to the world around us as an illusion. I struggled with this concept for a very long time. After all, when I bump my head or stub my toe, the objects I hit feel real enough. My hunger or thirst feels pretty real, too. How could any of this be an illusion?

What is real? Is perception reality? What about the hidden things? Are there things we cannot perceive that actually exist? What about dreams? We believe they exist because we experience them, but is there solid proof that they exist at all? Are dreams real? Technically, they are as real as the world we perceive around us (which is also a kind of dream).

The idea that we live in an illusion, or a waking dream, doesn't mean that we are no longer bound by physical laws—even if we wake up from it. Of course, we believe some things are immutable laws that actually are not, and when we grow in our awareness, we can see what those things are. One example is the idea that suffering is inevitable and largely unavoidable. That's not true at all. Likewise, at one time, the most brilliant minds in the world believed that moving faster than the speed of sound was impossible. That wasn't true—and it exemplifies the disconnect between perception and reality.

Our limited abilities to perceive or understand aspects of the universe we live in cause us to fill in the gaps with assumptions and imagination. We imagine that we know how dinosaurs looked. But in their book *All Yesterdays,* paleoartists John Conway and C. M. Koseman created renditions of ordinary modern-day animals based solely on their skeletons, and the results were hilarious and horrifying. It's natural for our minds to fill in the missing pieces. There is either too much information or not enough. We often misunderstand something we see or hear and create a false copy of that thing in our minds. I may see someone across a crowded room mouth the words "I love you" and remember that moment, but in reality, they just happened to look my way when they were saying "olive juice."

Numerous studies have been conducted to test the reliability of memory in all kinds of situations. It has been proven that eyewitness recollections are unreliable because of the many internal and external influences that can impact memory, stress and bias chief among them. Yet countless people are convicted in court based on unreliable testimony. The same thing can happen with our sense of self. We testify against ourselves in front of the judge in our minds, but our testimony is unreliable because we don't remember what really happened. Instead, we have a memory that vaguely resembles what happened, but is retouched with other memories, emotions, and biases.

If we can't be sure that what we observe is true, it must be an illusion. Famous magicians and illusionists can use our biases against us and trick our minds into thinking they've done something miraculous—like when David Copperfield made the Statue of Liberty disappear right before people's eyes. Most will know right away that it's a trick, but there is a little doubt somewhere in their minds while the mind tests the boundaries of what it believes is real and what it perceives. (I won't reveal the trick, but I promise the statue never moved.)

So far, we've looked at perceptual illusions. There are also psychological illusions. Learned biases are illusions that skew how we think about other people based on arbitrary criteria (skin color, gender identity, sexuality, national origin, religion, ability, appearance, finances, political ideology, social affiliations, and even geography). We can paint an entire picture of a person's life based on nothing more than a glance. When we filter information that way, is what we perceive, think, and feel real?

Likewise, relationships are full of illusions. "Wow! You think you know somebody, and then they go and do something like that!" Have you ever heard that expression? Have you ever experienced something like that? Did you know someone for a long time and thought you knew all about them, until they did something unexpected or betrayed your trust? Have you ever been surprised when a shy person did something bold? Have you ever done something that surprised even you? Do you know who you truly are, or is your self-image based on a thousand little thoughts created in your mind or given to you by others?

Sometimes when we listen to someone, they say something that we mishear or misunderstand. What we thought we heard was hurtful, and our mind instantly goes on the defensive. From then on, everything that person says is barbed. We might even tell that person off and suddenly dislike them. Then we find out we didn't hear what they said correctly, and we're embarrassed. We might make amends, or we might be too embarrassed and abandon the relationship entirely. Is that reality?

What if you're having a bad day? You don't feel well, or you start your day angry, and everyone you come into contact with irritates you. Maybe you're sad, and every song you hear is painful, too. Our moods can significantly influence our perceptions and how our minds filter information as it comes in. For instance, maybe one of those sad songs isn't sad at all, it's just at a slower tempo, and it feels sad to you in that moment.

I touched on this briefly in the second chapter when I was talking about perception. There are a lot of problems with perception. When we receive information, it has to go through different areas of the brain. The information is compared to what we've already experienced, and if it is new information, we make even more comparisons to help categorize what we've just received. Then we filter the information again with our biases, and then again with our emotions. By the time the information has been processed and we're consciously aware of it, milliseconds have gone by, and the initial event is over. It happens so quickly that we don't notice that what we are consciously considering is already history.

Imagine that a ball is flying through the air, coming straight for your head. First you see the ball, then you recognize it, and then process that it's moving toward you. Then you add those things together and realize that it's going to hit you in the head. Your hand flies up and deflects it, or catches it, if you've got the muscle memory or the extra time to process the physics. It all happens in a split second, in the blink of an eye. When it's over, the mind replays the whole thing again. *Where did the ball come from? Am I under attack? Is another ball going to come at my head? I could have been seriously injured!* We might experience fear and anger at the same time. Seconds later, the mind is doing what it does, and we feel the event as if it's happening *now*.

All of these examples so far deal with perception at some level. We can see that there are a lot of factors that can distort our perceptions, either in the moment or long after it. All of this happens in our thoughts. When we have thousands of thoughts going on all day, many at the same time and many of them conflicting, it becomes nearly impossible to know what is real and what isn't.

So, if we can't trust our senses, we can't trust our thoughts, and we can't trust our memories, is there anything about ourselves we can trust? Yes.

* * *

Dispelling the myth of "reality" by pointing out the flaws in our perceptions and minds is easy. However, another part of this world is an illusion that goes well beyond our perception. On one side is the concept of space-time, or time and space. We can measure time and space and get independent confirmation of the accuracy of our measurements. We can feel the passage of time and feel the matter and space around us. We live and die in a linear timeline. The universe isn't infinite, but has a quantifiable mass. These things are undeniable and easily proven.

The problem, though, has to do with origination. The origin problem has to do with how we are stuck in the perception of linear time. As science has progressed, we've learned that space-time isn't quite rigid; it's flexible. At least, that's the current thinking. That, too, is subject to change upon further investigation, but that is again perceptual. There are a lot of interesting theories about this at the intersection of physics, mathematics, and philosophy.

The only thing that is real and eternal is the energy that causes this universe to exist. This universe exists because eternity requires time, but time can't exist in eternity. The universe has a purpose, and because of that purpose, there is a construct. The only solid rule in the universe is that nothing can be added to it, and nothing can be taken away. The energy that exists is finite. From that, the other laws of the universe emerge. Within that, we are experiencing the universe.

But what are we? Since we are made up of the same energy as the universe, the matter and mass we are made of are the same as that of a galaxy, only smaller and in a different form. All the molecules and atoms that make up every part of us also exist in the dust and stars.

This energy of the universe has another quality that

can be felt when we try: intent. There is a will to that energy that is best described as the will to *Love*. When we tap into it, we can feel it in our minds with emotion, and in our bodies. It feels wonderful, like being in love. That's why it's often called *Love*.

We have a fantastic opportunity to experience this energy with self-awareness and emotion. The illusion is that we aren't the universe itself. The illusion is that we are tiny, powerless specs of dust within that universe. According to natural law, that illusion is easy to reinforce because we must experience the universe in this form. That law is part of the process, but no law in the universe forbids us from realizing the truth and exercising our full potential.

If none of this is real, you may ask, why can't we just zoom to another part of the universe or some other time? Well, we can, and we can't. The body we are currently inhabiting and responsible for is built into the construct that serves the purpose of *Love*. However, there are ways to have the spirit move anywhere in time and space and allow us to perceive that. I've had my own unique experiences, but it isn't something that I do, and I don't teach it. Some experienced teachers do and can guide you through transcendent experiences. There are some charlatans, too, but if we tune into the vibration[1] of *Love* and allow that

---

1   Sound waves, radio waves, light waves, and cosmic rays all vibrate at some frequency. Our brains produce waves of energy that are observable and measurable. The earth vibrates at a rate of about one cycle every three to five minutes. Gravitational waves travel across the entire universe for billions of years. Everything is moving, vibrating, or oscillating. There are often mystical qualities associated with how frequencies interact, synchronize, and harmonize with each other, but what we do know with certainty is that these vibrations exist.

energy to flow through us, we gain the wisdom to see people exactly as they are, and we will not be fooled so easily.

While I'm sure I could go on and on about this, I think the best way for you to understand it is to have you experience it for yourself. If you'd like to see the universe as it truly is, then clear away the fear in your mind, get all those random thoughts quiet, and tame the mind into accepting the truth. The latter was the most challenging part for me, but it can be done. When we have calmed our minds and brought our spirits to the forefront, we become in tune with the energy of *Love*. In this way, we have conscious contact with *Love* and can access the wisdom obscured by the illusion, like a giant statue obscured by the magician.

Another Thought about Perception

Let's look at something to demonstrate how our brains work and how perception and reality don't usually match. You may have seen these exercises on social media, in your email, or on a website, but they're fun and demonstrate how our brains can fill in gaps or miss things completely.

Aoccdrnig to smoe rscheearch, it deosn't mttaer waht oredr the ltteers in a wrod are in; the olny iprmoetnt tihng is taht the frist and lsat ltteres are at the rghit pclae. The rset can be a tatol mses, and you can sitll raed it wouthit a porbelm. Tihs is bcuseae we do not raed ervey lteter by istlef but the wrod as a wlohe.

Here's another one. Count every *F* in this sentence:

FOR EVERY FOURTH OF A DOLLAR,
THERE ARE TWENTY-FIVE CENTS, WHICH
CAN BE MADE UP OF FIVE NICKELS.

How many did you count? Four? Five? The answer is six. You probably got it right if you've seen something like this before. But the brain doesn't really process the word *of*, so there is a tendency to skip that *F* when counting the letters.

One more. Read the following words out loud:

A

BIRD

IN THE

THE BUSH

Did you say, "a bird in the bush"? Or did you say the extra "the" in the set of words?

These little demonstrations illustrate how the brain takes shortcuts with perception. It's really about efficiency over accuracy, because if we have the basic context, we can probably fill in most of the gaps and still make sense of what we see. However, the kind of perceptual reality we want to focus on when we're dealing with spiritual matters is notably different.

As with the above exercises, when we hear someone speak or we read a message, our brain starts trying to fill in the gaps. The accuracy of this process depends on how well we understand the underlying context, but it may also be influenced by our mood, state of mind, or our ability to focus on the message itself.

It's certainly one thing to point out the flaws in our perceptions, but it's another thing to do something about it. What can we do, and how does this relate to our spiritual self? It comes down to how we perceive ourselves and what we've based that perception on. I like to paint, and I like the paintings I've made. A long time ago, when I would try to paint, I hated what I made. I decided that I was not a painter or an artist, and I decided I would never try again. So, what changed? I'm not comparing myself to anyone else now, and I'm no longer invested in the outcome. I just keep painting until the image makes sense to me. It truly doesn't matter to me if anyone else likes the painting. It might be different if someone hired me to make a painting for them, but that's beside the point. In my case, I paint pictures because I enjoy the process. It's like a meditation for me. If it comes out looking like the subject, that's great. But it doesn't matter if it doesn't, because the object of my painting was just to paint. I was already successful the moment I started.

I can apply this to the rest of my life, too. I find joy in just being. My existence is the canvas. Things like interacting with people, studying art and history, reading books, and listening to music are my paints. My mind, my words, and my body are my brushes. In concert, these things create pictures in my life. It doesn't matter how the pictures turn out; the art of living is the true reward.

Long ago, I had a hard time with the way I perceived myself. I was full of conflict, doubt, bitterness, and self-loathing. But I didn't want to hate myself. I wanted to love myself, and I wanted to like who I was. So, I looked for validation from everyone but myself. I tested relationships to see if they'd break, or if the person would stay with me despite how messed up I believed I was. My self-esteem and self-loathing were so bad that I couldn't trust anyone who seemed to like or love me. In my mind, they were either stupid or trying to manipulate me.

It was an awful way to live, and I was always miserable. Even when I was being gregarious and funny, I hurt inside, and the more I got people to like me, the more I hated myself for being a fraud. However, the problem wasn't me, and it wasn't them. My perceptions were causing me to feel the way I did. I assumed everything I thought or believed about myself was probably true, when in fact, none of it was true at all.

It was difficult to break my dependency on my perceptions, and I still work on that every day. After all, we live in a society built around self-image, and we believe that how people perceive us is extremely important. We also think that our perceptions of others are important.

The game-changer for me was learning not to take anything personally. I had to work at it, but eventually, I realized that what anyone else says or does is never about me. How could it be? Their perception of me is so incomplete that it cannot be true. What someone thinks about me is just what they think about an image of me they have created in their minds. That image is built on assumptions and flawed perceptions with a lot of gaps filled in, or it has been changed to fit what they want me to be for them.

When I first started thinking about this, I thought, "Well, if I act like a jerk to someone, and then they think I'm a jerk, isn't that a true perception?" But when I look at that question, I think about all the people who treat others poorly, but are still admired—even by the people they abuse. It's really about perception. When we are bound to our perceptions, we will gladly see what we want to see, and we will work hard to make other people see what we want them to see. This is going on all around us; everyone is doing the same thing. So, how could we possibly know who we all are?

Now that I am aware that my perceptions are based on incomplete and often biased information, I can pull my energy back and invest it somewhere else. If someone tells me I'm ugly, so what? If someone tells me I'm magnificent, so what? Am I either of those things? Perhaps to them—but to me, I am what I am. I am *Love*; I am energy playing at life in this form. I'll say more about this in the chapter on judgment.

Chapter Four: *Self*

"Γνῶθι σεαυτόν (Know thyself)."
— Ancient Greek maxim

Know Thyself

Getting past our perception of self—or the ego—is an essential part of spiritual awakening. Until we ask the question, "Is this all that I am?", the ego is the core of our self-awareness. Whom we think we are changes—sometimes subtly, sometimes dramatically—as we progress through life.

Sigmund Freud was an early pioneer of psychoanalysis. Many of Freud's theories and methods have been criticized during the past century, but some of the concepts he coined are very useful. Freud imagined the human personality to be divided into three separate parts or roles: the id, ego, and superego.

The id is the part that is concerned with our most basic needs and animal instincts. The id is chaotic and driven by desire, seeking only pleasure and gratification.

The superego might equate to what we think of as our conscience; it is the judge that governs by the rules of society, community, and family. We derive our unconscious sense of right and wrong, morals, and ethics from the superego. It attempts to restrain the impulses of the id with its guidelines.

The ego is what we typically think of as the *self*, or our personality. Of the three, the ego is our conscious mind, where the id and superego often wrestle for control. The ego is the mediator, not only between the impulsive id and the restrictive superego, but of the perceived reality around us.

Of course, this is all happening in one mind. And we can see that there is merit to Freud's analogies by observing our own behavior. For example, our baser impulses might lead us to binge on food, sex, or drugs. The superego, or judge, compares that behavior to the rules or moral code and passes its judgment. In the middle is our conscious mind, weighing the consequences (guilt) against the reward (satisfaction). When we give in to the desire, the judge will impose itself, and if we have broken our internal law, we will feel guilty. We may have even broken the laws of society.

The brain is an organ within the animal body. It has many functions, but its most important purpose is facilitating survival. We learn how to satisfy our needs for survival by finding food and shelter, and by finding a mate to perpetuate the species and increase our numbers, so that together we can improve our chances of survival. Regardless of how civilized and modern we may have become, the brain will still do what it is supposed to do and send signals to other parts of the brain and body.

A long time ago, humans were just like any other social animal. We were wild, hunted in packs, attacked other humans to take from them, and roamed around searching for food. As the species evolved and developed language, we began to make rules that increased the chances of survival. Eventually, societies formed, and tribes began communicating, trading, or warring with other tribes. As our species evolved to create societies and laws, so did the brain. The brain has evolved to learn and apply the moral code established by the collective. Religions and governments were then formed to codify and enforce these rules.

Our minds are very much like our society in general. We have our own moral code, rules, and personal law within our thoughts. We adopt the code mandated to us by our religions and governments and augment it with more regulations and laws. For example, it's legal and acceptable in many societies and religions to drink alcoholic beverages, but we may personally decide it is immoral. We may even judge others by our internal laws, though there is little we can do to enforce them or punish those who violate them.

Our internal law is flexible, too. It changes when our ideals change. If we join and espouse a religion, many things we thought were okay may no longer be acceptable. Or if we were brought up to believe in the moral code of a religion, we may change our views when we reach adulthood, and our moral code becomes less rigid.

The animal instinct, the moral judge, and the conscious observer make up the core of our personality, but not our identity. Our personality is how we behave and relate to others (and we can have different personalities with different people or groups). Our identity is our perception of what makes us ourselves. Many other influences and thoughts go toward who we think we are as a person. There are so many things inside and outside our minds that define who we are as a personality. We believe things about ourselves based on our history or performance and our desires and wishes.

As humans, we each have many roles that we play. We are the biological offspring of two other humans. We may be a sibling, a parent or grandparent, a friend, a lover, a worker, a boss, or a neighbor. There are names for all kinds of relationships, activities, and jobs. I can be many different things all at once. Which one defines who I am? Am I what I do?

How do you know who you are? You have a name, but is that who you are? You have a body; is that who you are? You live in specific circumstances; does that define who you are? Maybe you've had a career most of your life; is that who and what you are? What about all of our experiences; is that who we are? Is it a bit of everything, or just some things? What about my personality? Is that who I am?

When we are little children, the concept of "I am" is utterly foreign to us. It just doesn't matter. Being self-aware isn't yet expected of us—at least, not until we can speak. We then learn about all the roles that grownups play, and we make believe with our very powerful imaginations. We pretend that we are other people—maybe someone from a book or a TV show, or perhaps even someone we know. We might even dress up and entertain the adults. "Who are you?" one might ask. "I'm a wizard!" the child says.

As we grow a little older, things get a bit more complicated. The older people around us don't know how powerful their words are, so they don't realize what they are doing when they tell us that we are good or bad, smart or stupid, pretty or ugly. We begin to compete for attention, and that brings criticism and judgment. Now we might feel great, so-so, or not good enough.

When we are teenagers, we see other people about our age who are "cool" and popular, and we think they are amazing, so we want to be like them and hope we can have what they have. If we believe our situation is terrible, we may be desperate to be someone else, so we act our way through, trying to impress the right people. Or maybe it's just the opposite, and we hate ourselves or everyone else and push people away.

The topic of self-perception is broad enough for several college courses and mountains of books. There are so many little thoughts, ideas, and dreams that go into the makeup of who we think we are that it's impossible to keep up.

All these thoughts and ideas bouncing around in our minds constantly alter and confuse our perceptions of *the self*. The way we perceive ourselves and see others can change based on our mood or how we feel physically. Have you ever thought, *That person is not who I thought they were,* or maybe *I guess they weren't my friend after all?* Have you ever wondered if anyone has thought that of you?

The truth is that creating a solid identity in the world is difficult and often impossible. There are just too many variables. We may want to get someone to like us, and we try to guess what we can do or say to make that happen, even if that means we go against our integrity. Of course, there are no guarantees that our efforts will be rewarded, or if they are, that it will be what we hoped for.

When we don't know ourselves, or perhaps despite it, we let others define who we are. In this age, this is aggravated by social media. So many people are begging for approval, constantly tweaking their persona to get more likes and followers. They may scroll through comments and agree with someone else's criticism, believe it, and then change how they behave and think about themselves. People can be cruel for cruelty's sake, and their target may willingly ingest that poison.

Think about a time when someone said something critical or mean to you, and it hurt your feelings. Did you believe them? Did you wonder if you deserved to be hurt like that? Did you do something to change because of it? Did you get angry and want to hurt them back? Did you do so?

Earlier, we looked at the inner judge and how it will use anything to keep us from realizing who we really are. As we quiet our thoughts and minds, the judge holds less and less power over us, and we become free to just be rather than play roles to impress the people around us.

One of the many beautiful things that happens in developing spiritual freedom is freedom from the ego. I am no longer the center of my cosmos. I know myself, and I have no need or desire to prove it to anyone. I am who I am.

In the Book of Exodus in the Old Testament of the Bible, Moses is about to head back down from Mount Horeb after conversing with God, who had taken the form of a burning bush. Moses wants to ensure that he can speak with authority when he tells the Israelites who sent him. He wants to know what name to give if he is asked. God replies, "I am who I am."

I am who I am. You are who you are. Once you become aware of and accept your divinity, that's all you need: just to *be*—unapologetically. When we allow ourselves to be conduits of unconditional *Love*, our ego lets go of the wheel and takes the back seat as a passenger. When we no longer let the ego drive who we think we are, we are free to express our true selves (we are *Love*) in any situation. That is what it is like to live in the present, the *now*.

Our ego has developed in a way that prevents it from being able to function in the present moment. The ego is constantly rehashing or rewriting our past or dreaming of ways to manipulate our future. When the ego is aware of the present moment, it takes only an instant before it starts comparing it to the past and contemplating the future. *What is this like, and how will it affect me?* That's what the ego does with any given moment. Taken a step further, by the time the ego has evaluated something from the present, it's already past.

Since we are timeless by our true nature, now is the only moment that exists. In our realm of space-time, things have happened, and things will happen—but past and future are meaningless for eternal beings. As we are eternal beings having a temporal human experience, we aren't going to separate the two, nor should we. When we live in this moment, this now, we are our most connected with our true identity. That makes living in time a lot of fun!

To live in the now is to live without fear or regret. We have forgiven the past, and we are sure that tomorrow will be just as it should be. We gain a powerful sense of perception and quickly find the opportunities we seek, or those that will help us accomplish our goals. We do not fear failure, because we are glad for those opportunities to reinforce the skills that have gotten us to this moment.

This is pretty important stuff. To *truly know* yourself has radical implications for your spiritual and even emotional freedom. The first step for me was learning to love myself unconditionally, to feel that love, and to commit to the practice. It didn't matter that I wasn't quite sure who or what I truly was; that would come in time. Instead, I needed the power of unconditional love to free me from the criticism and condemnation that had always been a part of my personality. I needed to be able to overcome self-accusations and self-doubt and reclaim my personal power.

Without that freedom, my ego and my habit of self-deprecation would have been allowed to keep throwing out lies and doubt to obscure what I am inside. I now know that I was subconsciously asking myself many times a day, "Who am I? Who am I supposed to be?" Then my ego and the thousand voices (thoughts) in my mind would all offer their opinions. Without even knowing what was happening, I was stuck in a loop. I believed what people said about me— their opinions, praise, criticism, and even their insults. I believed in the ideal of what I hoped I might be, but I also believed the accusations and insults I heaped upon myself. Sadly, this is the way most of us live for most of our lives. We are constantly stuck in an identity crisis because we're continually trying to figure out who or what we're supposed to be for other people and for ourselves, all at the same time.

When I began to try to seriously love myself, and when that love started to sink in, the transformation was amazing. I found that who and what I am is not a personality; I am a spirit. I am energy. I am connected to everything that exists. I am the same as the trees, the rocks, the oceans, and the animals. I am the same as you.

I didn't surrender my personality when this process took hold. I just changed my perspective to look at the core, the essence of my being. It doesn't matter what my personality is. It doesn't matter what anyone thinks about me—if they like me or hate me. Instead, I now view my personality as a means of communication. That is its sole purpose.

I am the way I am because that is how I *want* to be. Certain things require absolute acceptance. I must accept that my body and brain have good and not-so-good days. I must accept that I have to deal with my mood disorder. But that doesn't mean that *I am* that disorder. It's just something that needs to be dealt with constructively. Again, some days are better than others.

I have developed a certain level of detachment. I now separate the different facets of my being into their distinct roles. My personality is just my style; it's how I communicate with others. I don't need to force it or try to be something or someone I'm not. What difference does it make? It's impossible to please everyone, so why not just be what I want to be: authentic?

That detachment works both ways, too. I have to be detached from the judgment of others. Nobody else can experience being me, so why would I accept their judgment of what I'm supposed to be? I'm not dismissing their opinions out of hand; there can be valuable feedback in those opinions. But I'm not going to take them in and then change myself just to be more favorable to them. That's just being manipulative and fake.

Another way to say this is that I detach from all judgment of my personality. This allows my ego to ignore judgment and enjoy less stress. Free from the stress of constantly reevaluating myself, my ego can be useful and help me express my joy and gratitude. Ironically, I've found that if I don't try to impress someone, they're much more likely to be impressed by my authenticity, and they in turn are more likely to be authentic themselves.

There is an amazing benefit to knowing and accepting yourself: you can interact with anyone fearlessly. It doesn't matter if someone judges you, because that's their thing; good for them. Today, I rarely notice if someone is judging me—and when I do, I remind myself that their opinion of me is none of my business. Since I'm not judging them, though, it's not likely that I will be paying attention to that anyway.

I love myself unconditionally, and that means I love myself without judgment. This gives me so much freedom, because I can express my personality however I feel like it. It isn't that I'm constantly changing and inconsistent; that would just confuse people. It's that I get to shape myself in whatever way feels good. My evolution is in my own hands. I can ask myself, "Am I how I want to be today?" If the answer is yes, I go about my day. If not, I'm just as happy working on whatever aspect of my personality I want to change.

That control, that power, grants me the knowledge of who I truly am. Imagine that you are a sculptor. You have an idea, a vision of what you want a sculpture to look like, and how you hope it will make people feel. You get busy molding the clay, pushing and pinching, scraping and shaping. As you go along, your vision changes because you see something in the clay you didn't imagine before. You see something that makes you feel better. So, you alter what you're doing and go with what the clay tells you. Eventually, you finish your sculpture, polish it or paint it, and get it ready to share with others. Though you started with an idea, you didn't fully know what the end result would be—but at every step, you knew exactly what was in your hands. Even before the sculpture took its final form, you *knew* what it was.

It's the same way with personality. Our personalities will change over time. We make adjustments and fine-tune them here and there. But when we are aware of and in control of that process, we know who we are all the time. With unconditional love comes magnificent confidence to exist as you see fit—not how others would have you to be.

Mindfulness

The word *mindfulness* is frequently used in a spiritual context. I touched on this earlier, but I want to go into more detail about self-knowledge. Mindfulness is knowing who, what, and where you are in this moment. It excludes contemplation of the past or future and concentrates instead on the *now*. This is the only moment that exists, and *now* is the only time that matters.

Mindfulness meditation can go a long way in bringing our awareness of self to the forefront of our minds. This goes beyond ego, because the ego is always trying to compare past, present, and future to get a sense of who we ought to be—or more accurately, who we pretend to be. By its very nature, the ego cannot be in the moment. Remember, the ego is who and what we *think* we are and the persona we want to project. The problem is that the ego is wrestling with what we desire versus what we can logically obtain, our internal moral code, the fear that we might get caught doing something others consider wrong, or the fear of our dishonesty being discovered. There are thousands of calculations the ego has to make to keep the pieces of our personality together.

We tend to act differently with different people. There are some with whom we are more reserved. There are those with whom we cut loose and act silly. There are those whom we may let see what we think is the *real us*. We wear many masks for many different audiences and occasions. This is one of the main reasons we need to tame our thoughts and quiet our minds. Even though the ego is operating in the present, it is never in the moment, because the thoughts it is controlling and moving around in our brains are spread out across time and relationships.

When we meditate mindfully, we quiet our thoughts. With time and practice, mindful meditation will bring our mind into the awareness of a single moment where no thought can exist. Our attention focuses on the gap between thoughts. In this gap, we are aware of ourselves as we truly are, without labels, masks, judgments, or assumptions. In this gap comes clarity. It isn't a thought, but a feeling and knowledge. We just *know* who we are in that moment.

There are many teachers, guides, books, videos, and websites available that teach mindfulness meditation much better than I can. However, it isn't a complicated meditation. The simplest form that I use often is a breathing exercise. Find a quiet, relaxing place where you won't be disturbed for a few minutes. Get in a comfortable position, sitting in a chair or on the floor with legs crossed. Breathe in deeply through your nose (if possible), and slowly exhale through your mouth. Find a comfortable pace and rhythm of breathing. You want to be relaxed, but not light-headed. Focus your concentration on your breathing—in and out— and feel the air moving in and out of your lungs. Study the sensations in your lungs as you breathe. Once you've established your rhythm, say "om" over the entire exhale. Let the air you exhale carry the word out. When you breathe in, focus on the sensation of your chest expanding and the air moving into your lungs.

There are two points where we can find the gap, between inhale and exhale. Just before you exhale, you can find a small gap. After you've finished your "om," there is a larger gap just before you inhale. I like to imagine that my exhale is a slide on a playground, and I am the "om" sliding down my breath. In the end, I slip into the gap that is this moment, and as much as I can, I empty my mind of most thoughts. As I continue, that gap gets wider, and I can stay in it longer. The more frequently I practice, the longer I can stay in the gap.

The experience of this gap—the awareness of the *moment*—stays with you. The experience is something that you feel, and while you may think of ways to describe that feeling, it is not a thought. That feeling is very powerful because it allows us to see ourselves from a different perspective. We can only exist in this moment. Our thoughts go back and forth in time, but they cannot pull our authentic selves with them—only an image created by the ego. In time and with practice, our need to project our ego diminishes. We discover that the image isn't real, but something we've created so we can communicate with other people. It's like a house that is painted yellow. The color is what the house presents as its personality, but in reality, it is simply a house.

Our outward appearance and the qualities of our personality are like the yellow paint on the house. Some people only see a yellow house, but others see a two-story house, a big or small house, or maybe a house with a chimney. Some people may make assumptions about what is in the house and who lives there. The same is true for how people view us; everyone sees something different.

Some know us and have a good idea of what we look like on the inside. Others make assumptions and create their own images of us.

There are a few people, though, who look past the exterior. They know that what they are looking at is special. They are like builders and architects; they know what makes a house a house. They know not to make assumptions from what they can see on the outside. The few who have found their way into conscious awareness of the moment, who are in tune with their connection to the universe and are filled with and radiating unconditional *Love*, see nothing but light. They see you and me just as we are, without expecting or assuming anything else.

I have become like this, and I know that if you want to, you can, too. This is the ultimate form of knowing yourself. When you look at your reflection or contemplate yourself, you see nothing but light.

Chapter Five: *Faith*

"Now faith is the certainty of things
hoped for, a proof of things not seen."
— Hebrews 11:1

A Matter of Trust

My Faith is built on a single principle: I trust that now is exactly as it should be. That doesn't mean that my environment or circumstances are always painless or ideal. It simply means that my true self—my being—is not bound to my circumstances. I trust that my connection to my *Source* will give me all the wisdom I need to stay connected, and that my joy is assured.

There are times when something in life demands our attention. Perhaps my family and I have to move because the landlord is giving the house we are renting to their child. Moving is troublesome and expensive. What will we do? Where will we go? Can we find a place that meets our wants and needs in time? How am I going to make this work? This is all egocentric thinking.

Some people might say that this is the kind of problem you want to have, because in this example, we at least have the means to go somewhere. We will have food and shelter. What else do we truly need? But what if it's something that isn't a luxury problem? Suppose we lose our income and can't afford any place? What if one or all of us get sick with a fatal illness? How much harder is it to focus on the Light with such dire circumstances demanding my attention?

The real problem with *problems* is the misplaced attention that the mind gives them. Any problem can be broken down: What is the problem? What are the consequences? What are the alternatives? What can I do about it? Can I deal with this on my own, or should I ask for help? Does knowing what caused the problem make a difference? If we can break a problem down into bite-size chunks, we can release a good portion of our attention, stay focused on *Love*—or the *Source*—and regain our clarity of mind, freedom from worry, and Faith.

You may be wondering what good it will do to divert any attention that could be used to solve the problem. That's a good question with a straight answer. Problems are inevitable. There are always puzzles to be solved and accounts that need to be balanced; that's just part of being human. However, problems only need to be given the amount of attention required to solve them, and not an iota more.

How do you know how much attention is enough? That is the beauty of being at peace and in tune with *Love*. It isn't that you gain any new wisdom that you didn't already have; it's that you are more aware of the wisdom you already possess. In all likelihood, you already have the solutions to the problems before they even arise. But if we are totally focused on the problem itself, it is hard to draw on our inner wisdom, and we try to invent solutions beyond our awareness.

Having to move out of a house when I wasn't prepared for it is something that has happened (more than once) to my family. I wasn't ready mentally or financially, and I knew it would cost a lot more than we had. I got frustrated and angry—but mostly, I was afraid. I scrambled for options, trying to find a new place. Many applications were denied because of some poor decisions I had made long ago. I grew progressively more anxious, and I felt guilty because I feared my past actions would now hurt my family. They would suffer because of something foolish I'd done fifteen years ago. My fear manifested in so many negative emotions, and I started to hate myself.

Then I remembered who and what I am. I am not my past, and though decisions and behaviors from long ago may still haunt me today, I am not those things. I must deal with whatever comes, regardless of the source. Some things that might hurt us come from the randomness and chaos around us. Some things don't happen because of what we have done, but just because everything is always in motion.

I realized that I had allowed myself to be infected by *Fear*, and it was manifesting all kinds of thoughts and emotions that further blocked the flow of *Love* within and through me. My guilt and anger were doing nothing to solve the problem, but were only adding to it. Not only was I giving too much attention to the problem at hand, I'd also shifted my attention to my fear. I was miserable, and I was denying my family the *Love* that usually flows through me all the time.

When I stepped back and moved all my attention back to the *Source*, I allowed *Love* to flow through me again.

I recognized that the things compounding the problem (my past) didn't matter. There was nothing I could do about it, and though my options were somewhat limited, I still had options. That gave me something to be grateful for, and that gratitude calmed my mind. I also knew from experience that I had made a mistake when I didn't fall back on Faith from the outset. I could have made a quick inventory of all that we had—our resources, of course, but also our joy and love. I could have put even more focus on the *Source* to better see the landscape and see the problem as an opportunity instead.

Better late than never, I did just that. I stepped back and meditated. I considered what we had materially and realized that we were so blessed and privileged that there was no problem at all. It was merely a shift. Instead of panicking, I could pull back from the problem and see opportunities I would have missed had I kept my nose pressed to the wall of fear and worry I was manifesting. What happened next was a sense of calm and peace. I had my joy, I released my fear, *Love* resumed its flow, and the solution materialized on its own. We only had to accept the answer, and now we live in a home that better suits our wants and needs.

Faith is what keeps us grounded and strengthens our connection to the *Source*. Living in *Love* carries us through when we slip back into *Fear*, and it brings us back to joy. Faith is a lifeline, a buoy, and a safe harbor in the storm.

Throughout my many years of study and practice, I have read a lot of material about manifesting through intention. This is sometimes called the Law of Attraction. It is real, and it does work, but I think it is also a slippery slope. First, focusing on manifesting or attracting what we want can be a prelude to greed. Greed is nothing but a form of *Fear*—a lack of *Love*. I'm not saying that manifesting and attracting favorable situations or things is inherently wrong, but I think spiritual setbacks can and do arise if our expectations are misaligned with reality.

I'm bringing up the Law of Attraction and manifesting through intention because those things are not separate from Faith, but are derived from it. Let's look again at the story I just told you. How is it that I manifested a better place for us to live? Was it through intention? Was it that I somehow pulled ethereal power from the *Source* and manipulated reality into conforming with my desires? Surely not! What happened is that when I plugged back into the *Source,* my mind was in a whole other zone. I wasn't thinking about my lot in life; instead, I appreciated the *Love* that flowed through me, and I enjoyed that bliss. I pulled my attention away from the problem and redirected that energy into awareness. It's like trying to find your keys with foggy glasses on; you will find nothing until you remove the glasses and restore your ability to see clearly. You can pull back and see more from a broader perspective, and finding what you are looking for becomes much easier.

In practicing Faith, we can trust that our senses are clearer and our wisdom is true when we keep our attention on *Love* itself. Faith allows us to see that we exist now, and that circumstances do not define us. A prisoner isn't going to manifest an open gate through intention if all the prisoner is focused on is the gate. On the other hand, a prisoner may manifest their joy, despite the circumstances of being in prison, and with *Love* as the point of focus, may be able to see opportunities to hasten the opening of the gate. And when we live in that state of grace, the gate and the fence don't matter. Bliss is bliss, no matter where you are.

Faith doesn't give me the power to attract anything I might want. Instead, it allows me to move through time and space in a way that helps me to see those things clearly and from afar. That way, I can alter my steps and timing to be available for the right opportunities. When I remain in a state of grace, I can rely on Faith to be my guide and trust that where I am at this moment is exactly where I need to be.

What about the times when the circumstances of life are unavoidably painful? There are a few ways I can answer this question. First, there is a threshold we may cross on our path to and through enlightenment, where one's relationship with the world is no longer a source of either pain or joy. This is acceptance in its fullest power. You become impervious to the slings and arrows of outrageous misfortune. But if we aren't there yet, or we are in a moment of crisis, the ever-present anchor of Faith will—if we don't let go of the line—keep us within reach of the power and wisdom of the *Source*.

Even in the midst of great pain (physical or psychological), Faith can remind us that there must always be balance. Pain can be a motivator and a teacher. There is no good or bad about being in pain or bliss. At times, we may have a reason (whether it is reasonable or not) to dip into pain, or even bathe in it. There are times when I willingly allow pain or fear to come in. In my Faith, I know that I am doing so of my own free will. I know and trust that I am making a bargain, and a balance will be struck. I know that I will receive something in exchange for the pain. The question is, though, is it worth it? Am I trading my joy for something I need, or a lesson I've already learned? It would be hard to tell, since pain and fear tend to blind us to reality and spiritual awareness.

Faith will ultimately pull us back to our natural state of grace and *Love*, no matter what emotional or psychological roller coaster we might find ourselves on.

Finding Faith or Building It

I want to dissect a quote from the New Testament of the Bible. The context is a discussion of Israel's rejection of the Gospel of Christ. Within that discussion is a line about Faith that stands out: "So then faith cometh by hearing, and hearing by the word of God" (Romans 10:17, King James Version). This verse is saying that Faith comes from what is heard, and what is heard comes from the word of God. In this way, Faith begins with what we hear through our perception (through our ears, or reading with our eyes or fingers), and ends with how we process the words with our minds. Whether what we hear is the word of God is relative and subjective. These words you are reading now in this book may be the word of God for you—or perhaps they aren't. Unless and until we begin plugging directly into the *Source*, perceptual input will have to do.

Words are ideas, and ideas are given life when we receive them. The word of God starts as an idea that we ingest, but it also lives natively in our minds. We are made of *Love,* and our true nature is to be the word of God. As we travel and grow on our spiritual journey, we hear that word inside us louder and clearer.

Our Faith is activated when we hear the right words— words that resonate. There is a spark that lights a flame. If we acknowledge the flame, we can grow it into a brilliant light. In this way, we have found our Faith. Once it is found, we can cultivate it, and it will grow. We can build our Faith by exercising it and experiencing the resulting flow of *Love* through ourselves.

I do not believe that our Faith can shrink—only that we can shrink away from our Faith. I see my Faith as an extension of my spiritual self. It is an attachment between the *Source* and me. Sometimes, my mind causes my end of the attachment to wave around like a flag in a breeze. I can then lean on my Faith and rest, or I can pull myself into the *Source* through the power of Faith.

I've heard some people describe their Faith as "strong" or "weak," and I have sometimes used these words myself. But I don't think that's quite accurate. Faith is Faith; it is unchanging. Instead, our awareness of and connection to our Faith can be nearer or farther away, giving the impression of a weaker or more vital force of Faith.

Faith and belief are often conflated as a single concept, but they are not the same. Belief is malleable. Belief will change over time in the face of (or despite) new evidence or ideas. Scientists and philosophers once firmly believed that the earth is flat. Once better observations and calculations were made, the belief changed, although some still denied the evidence and continued to believe that. Belief is only loosely coupled with reality or truth.

Faith is rooted in trust. I may have faith that what I believe is true, even though it isn't, but in this case, it is the *belief* that is mistaken and not the faith. This is a philosophical and psychological idea.

When I emphasize "Faith," I mean something that isn't about trust in a belief. I'm talking about knowledge.

My Faith reminds me of what I know to be true—not what I *think* might be true. I know that I am. I know what and who I am, and I know why I'm here. I know that only this moment exists, and that in the time it takes to process and consider it, it's already gone. I know what it feels like to be a conduit for *Love,* and I know what that means in the biggest picture. When I forget these things or get confused by doubt, Faith brings me back around and reminds me of what I know to be true. Conversely, I know that what I *believe* about things may or may not be true. I know that my thoughts and perceptions create my beliefs, but my Faith is simple and unchanging.

* * *

Perhaps a pertinent question is "What does Faith do? How does Faith align with a higher state of awareness and enlightenment?"

As I mentioned, Faith is a byproduct of *Love.* Like a branch sprouting off a tree trunk, Faith extends the tree. Faith allows us to move back and forth, in and out of the *Source,* and through varying degrees of awareness.

Faith also holds the memory of our communion with God and our oneness with *Love.* Faith is the bridge that keeps our being (made from the energy of *Love*) connected to the *Source,* and spans the gulf created when we lack awareness of our true selves. In this way, *Faith* is knowing where home is.

As we practice quieting and aligning our thoughts and taming the mind, the knowledge of truth we become aware of gets placed in Faith, and our attachment to and reliance on Faith grows. I don't believe that I am one with God (the *Source*, *Love*); I *know* I am. When I don't feel it as strongly as I'd like, it is Faith that reminds me of what is true, and that assurance is a blessing.

* * *

This book is an extension of my Faith. Sitting at my keyboard and putting the words from my heart onto the page is an exercise in Faith. I don't know if many will read this, or if anyone will get anything out of it; that isn't up to me. But I have Faith that what I am doing strengthens my connection and brings me closer to the *Source*. I have Faith that by improving this connection and ensuring the flow of *Love* through me, I will be present in the moment and available for someone who will benefit from the light of the flame I carry, but do not own.

I know that every spirit who connects to the *Source* brings us all closer together and adds to the joy of the entire universe. When we grow in that spirit, I know we radiate *Love* that impacts everyone and everything around us. Have you ever been out of sorts—depressed or angry or jealous or afraid—and some stranger walks by? They just move past without a word, but it catches your attention. Just their proximity was enough to make your mood change. I have seen this happen countless times, where one person radiating *Love* drives away tension and fear and changes the mood of a whole room full of people.

I have faith in *Love's* ability to drive out *Fear*, like light chases away the darkness. There is a Bible verse that I am quite fond of that relates to this: "There is no fear in love; but perfect love casteth out fear: because fear hath torment. He that feareth is not made perfect in love. We love because He first loved us" (1 John 4:17-18, KJV). He is the *Source*; He is *Love*. *Love* can do nothing else but love what is created by it. We love it back because it is in our nature to do so. That is what our being is all about. But what we've become in our minds fights against it, because without that *Love*, there is *Fear*. This describes Faith, distilled into its purest form.

I have Faith that no matter what we're going through, no matter how hard the journey, and whether or not we ever become aware and realize it, we will unite with the *Source*.

Chapter Six: *Spirituality*

"The privilege of a lifetime is to become who you are."
— Carl Jung

What Does "Spiritual" Mean?

So far, I've mentioned some form of the word *spiritual* dozens of times, but what does that word mean? There are a couple of ways to define the word: either having to do with sacred, religious things, or with the spirit or soul. But still, what does it mean, and what is "spiritual awareness" or "spiritual awakening"?

To answer this, I need first to define *spirit*. That word, too, has many different definitions and ideas behind it. The word's origin is the Latin word *spirare*, which means "to breathe." Later, the term became *spiritus*, or "breath." A sibling word, *inspire*, is from the Latin *inspirare*, which means "to live into."

Our spirit is the breath and the life force of *Love* itself. It is the essence of the universe. This energy is in everything—every particle of existence. As humans, we can connect directly with that life force through the spirit within ourselves.

To be spiritual is to study and be focused on the spirit. Spirituality is a brain game, because it is the act of contemplating the intangible essence of our being. A spiritual awakening is that "ah-ha!" moment when our mind becomes aware of our own spirit's presence and our innate connection to the spirit of *Love*, that we are All One.

It would truly be amazing if having a spiritual awakening was a once-and-for-all event, but it usually isn't. It's more like starting a car. That initial bump gets the motor started, but it takes a bit more effort to keep the car going. It needs fuel, and it needs to be controlled by the driver.

Being spiritual is to practice spirituality in order to develop and maintain our conscious contact with the *Source*. The longer we practice it, the easier it is to maintain. But the work lies in changing our minds, quieting our thoughts, and tuning our perception to the vibrations of the *Source*—of *Love*.

* * *

Spiritual awareness comes when we have tamed our minds and know who we truly are. It comes with the experience of conscious contact with God. It gives us access to higher states of consciousness and allows us to know God, and to know that we are God.

Does this mean that to be in conscious contact with God all the time, we have to be spiritual all the time? I suppose that depends on the context. Spirituality isn't so much a way of thinking or behaving as it is a way of *being*. Since we all have a personal idea of what being spiritual is, it may not be evident at all to us if someone else is or isn't spiritual. No one can identify or define your spirituality for you. It is what you choose to make of it. To some degree, it's a proposition of "you'll know it when you see it." But there are guideposts you can identify to give you a hint of where you are along your journey. For me, the simplest way to feel spiritual is to accept and love myself just as I am in this and every moment.

Spirituality isn't a lifestyle, but a lifestyle can be spiritual. Spirituality isn't religious, but religion can be spiritual. The expression of your spirituality is yours to create, and it isn't rigid. You can change your behavior and rituals in whatever way enhances and reinforces your spirituality, and thereby, your conscious contact with the *Source*. Also, when we have that conscious contact with God, we are more aware of our connections with each other.

Chapter Seven: *Religion*

*"My religion is very simple. My
religion is kindness."*
— *The Dalai Lama*

Spirituality is Not Religion, But Religion Can Be Spiritual

Spirituality is compatible with just about any religion, but not all religions are compatible with spirituality. In other words, you can follow just about any religious doctrine and be spiritual, but some religious dogma can prevent the enjoyment of spirituality. You can be spiritual and also be religious, or not be religious. Neither is dependent on the other.

There are thousands of religions in the world. There are some, though, that are so dogmatic and rigid, so filled with fear, anger, hatred, and judgment, that their practice cannot allow conscious contact with God. In many cases, this is by design; anything created by human thought can be corrupted and used for selfish or manipulative purposes.

It would be unfair to paint all religions with the same brush. Religion can be an excellent aid to spiritual practice. Like any tool, though, it can be used for building or for tearing down; it just depends on the intent and the hand that wields it.

Perhaps one reason religion can be so volatile is that it

is so deeply personal. A lot of mental and emotional energy goes into understanding, obeying, and defending religious doctrine. It is often taught in the home from the day we are born. It isn't just something academic; it's baked into the very culture of our families and communities. Our religion is often practiced communally with our friends and family, or we become part of a community of believers on our own.

The association between religion and personal identity can run deep. If someone is asked what religion they believe in, the answer often begins with "I am," such as "I am Muslim" or "I am a Baptist." The words "I am" are a direct association with identity and can become the who and what of that person's idea of self.

It's essential to pry that association loose. Religion is something to *do*, not be. At the same time, I only mean to uncouple religion and identity and not discard one or the other. The reason is that religion is always open to interpretation, and the doctrine and practices can be different from place to place. Suppose I grew up attending a Baptist church in my hometown, but moved away and went to another church. In that case, I would have some difficulty reconciling the differences if my identity were intertwined with my understanding of the religion. However, if I decouple my identity from my religion, I don't have anything invested in how other groups practice it. I don't have to change anything about myself to try and fit in, and I don't have any anxiety about how other people think, feel, and act in regards to that religion. That way, I can still enjoy the practices and rituals without it interfering with my spirituality.

Once I understand religion as a tool to aid spiritual practice, I can also shed any judgment about the people of my religion, people of other religions, or people of no religion. In addition, I lose the need to defend my religion, because it isn't part of my identity any more than my postal code is. The more things we can disconnect from our identities, the better we become at not taking anything personally.

Chapter Eight: *Atheism*

*"We are all atheists about most of the
gods that humanity has ever believed in.
Some of us just go one god further."*
— *Richard Dawkins,* The God Delusion

Yes, Atheists Can Be Spiritual

Even though I use the word *God,* I do not mean to imply a supernatural or even an intelligent being. I speak of *Love* as the *Source* of creation. I speak of intention as the creative spark. However, I use these words to describe concepts related to the actual basic energy that makes up the universe around us.

Some people gain comfort from the idea that an intelligent supreme being is watching over us—one that gives purpose and meaning to life. In and of itself, there's nothing right or wrong with such beliefs. Problems only arise when such beliefs are used to manipulate, oppress, or otherwise abuse other people.

The spirituality I practice and teach has nothing to do with the supernatural. It is first and foremost psychological. It offers a way to consciously connect with the energy of the universe, to vibrate at the same frequencies as all of existence. There is nothing mystical or magical about it. Everything has spirit. However, we humans have an exceptional ability and opportunity to feel and connect with the energy within us—the energy I call "spirit." It is entirely independent of the existence or absence of any deities.

When I began this journey to personal spiritual freedom, I still held to Christian doctrine—albeit watered down a bit. The longer I practiced my spirituality, however, the less dependent I became on the necessity or even notion of God. I don't want to make this a treatise on my belief or disbelief in the existence of a god (or gods). It's a useless argument that cannot be won and is not worthy of the time or energy required to dispute it one way or the other. My point is that a belief in God is not necessary to achieve enlightenment or experience transcendence.

I can't explain how everything in the universe works; I wouldn't even try. I have had many experiences that I cannot explain—some miraculous—but that doesn't mean that no explanation exists. For instance, I have no idea how human consciousness can escape the confines of the brain and body. I likewise have no idea how a mind can see without eyes. I only know what I've experienced.

I am also open to the possibility that some of my inexplicable experiences were merely delusions. It doesn't matter to me if they were; the important thing is what I got out of it. I've had dreams that were so profound that they changed something inside me that I still carry to this day. Dreams are experiences in and of the mind. Most of us dream, but no one knows for certain how dreams work or what their function is; we have only theories.

The point is that the only requirement for spiritual

freedom is the willingness to love yourself and others without conditions, judgment, or expectations. Combined with action and patience, there is virtually no limit to the depth of spiritual awareness and connection you can achieve.

Part Two

Chapter Nine: *Fear*

*"Power is of two kinds. One is
obtained by the fear of punishment and
the other by acts of love. Power based on
love is a thousand times more effective and
permanent than the one derived from fear
of punishment."*

— *Mahatma Gandhi*

Fear is the Root of All Evil

If *Love* had an opposite, it would be *Fear.* When I use the word *Fear*, capitalized and italicized, I am referring to the absence of *Love.* We usually think of fear as being afraid of or worrying about something or someone. But some other negative states and emotions are also rooted in fear: grief, anger, hatred, resentment, prejudice, greed, envy, lust, and many other destructive traits.

Spiritual *Fear* is nothing but the absence or lack of spiritual *Love. Fear* does not really exist, but we can feel its emptiness mentally, emotionally, and physically. Another way to think of *Fear* is to compare it to darkness. *Darkness* is only a word describing the absence of light, but we can sense that absence, and thus we give it a name. Likewise, when the energy and power of *Love* are blocked, we feel that lack as some manifestation of *Fear.*

We are naturally fearless when we allow ourselves to be conduits of *Love* and radiate that energy. We may not be fully immune to the fear of the world, but we are very resistant to its effects.

When we witness the horrible things that people do to each other in the world, we may qualify those things as being "evil." We may feel that committing any of the seven deadly sins or breaking any of the Ten Commandments is evil. However we qualify such things, when we drill down deeper, it's plain to see that at the root of all "evil" is *Fear*.

To put it another way, if we are flowing with *Love*, there can be no *Fear*, nor any of its manifestations. *Love* is the light, and *Fear* is the darkness. Where one is, the other cannot be.

This world can be a terrifying place, dangerous and tragic. War is destructive, ruinous, and unnecessary. Natural disasters are likewise destructive, yet indiscriminate. Whether we are personally caught up in such a calamity or just strongly empathetic to others' suffering, fear, worry, and grief can creep in and disrupt or choke off the flow of *Love* energy within us. In times like these, it is helpful—if not essential—to take a step back, acknowledge our emotions and *Fear*, and then return to *Love* as soon as we can. Where there is *Love,* there is no *Fear*. In that state of mind and spirit, acceptance comes. Then, our *Fear* and worry subside with our ability to accept things just as they are (though not necessarily as we would have them be).

Hatred and Bigotry

It is often said that hate is the opposite of love. This isn't true, even when we're speaking strictly of emotions. I believe that indifference is a truer opposite of emotional love, as hatred, like love, requires passion and effort.

Hatred is rooted in *Fear*. It may be born of resentment, bigotry, intolerance, fear of "otherness," fear of loss, envy, and the like. There may be times when we see hatred as a benefit. I might say or feel, "I hate prejudice," "I hate injustice," or "I hate war." I may be passionate about that hatred and feel wholly justified in bearing those feelings. Who would argue with me and say it is wrong to hate such things? I cannot judge whether it is right or wrong, but I know it isn't helpful; it's hurtful, because it fuels the fire of anger, uses up valuable energy, and contributes to blockages that prevent the flow of *Love*.

Now, you might be wondering, "But how can you not hate abuse?", and you'd be asking a great question. This is getting into the semantics of the word *hate*. Here I am referring to a passionate, visceral emotion—not a degree of dislike. But even with the milder term of *dislike*, we need to be cautious and aware of the danger in our judgment.

What if someone abuses or otherwise injures me, or someone I care about? It's easy to feel passionate disgust toward them, but it doesn't do anyone any good. We might easily justify hatred of someone as a defense; hatred prevents us from feeling empathy or love for the target. We may hold on to those powerful negative emotions so that we don't slip up and allow ourselves to be vulnerable or abused by them again. Hatred is frequently just a refusal to offer love or forgiveness. Often, hating someone is merely the fear of being hurt by them. It puts up tall, thick walls to aid in our defense.

Bigotry is a form of hatred that may or may not be established by a personal experience. If we've had one or many awful experiences with members of a particular group, our innate biases may evoke hatred for that group as a whole. Often, bigotry is learned, taught to us by our elders or our community. We might even adopt the bigotry of a person or a group we want to get close to, in order to fit in. Regardless of the cause, bigotry is an insidious poison that builds up within us, inevitably spills out, and then infects others like a virus.

No matter what form hatred takes, it will destroy us if we harbor it inside us. Hatred is like a vat of boiling acid that fills itself with all the fear energy we feed into it. Several different kinds of fear may feed a single object of hate. The damage hate does to our minds can be devastating and difficult to repair.

Anger

I have a few questions for you: What makes you angry? Are you angry about something right now? Have you ever been angry about situations that don't affect you directly, or at people you don't know or have never met? Have you ever been so mad at someone you loved that you felt like you didn't love them anymore? Do you feel justified when you are angry with someone?

What is anger, anyway? There are variations in and degrees to what makes us angry, what emotions it makes us feel, and how we react. Regardless of the cause or the effect, anger is perhaps the most toxic emotional response we can have. No matter the cause or reason, anger is simply *Fear* that has been activated. Anger is a response to some form of *Fear*, and the power of its effect is directly proportional to the lack of *Love* (*Fear* with a capital *F*) filling and flowing through us. *Fear* stops the flow of *Love* through us like turning off a faucet—and anger, activated *Fear*, puts a lock on the valve.

The perceived power of anger comes from our mind's need to justify and defend the emotion. This is reinforced by a lifetime of validation from our family, social circles, community, and the world. We are taught what we should or shouldn't be angry about. It's easy to justify our anger because this is a very angry planet. Injustice and cruelty are all around us. Even on a more interpersonal level, the people around us can have a bad day and lash out at us, or at the very least, disappoint us.

Is anger "bad"? Not inherently—but it isn't good for us either. It's dangerous, too, to be trapped in duality. Bad is supposed to be the opposite of good; thus, we think if something or someone isn't good, then it or they must be bad. The problem is that "good" and "bad" are subjective, and the rules that judge good and bad vary from time to time and place to place. Ultimately, you are allowed to define for yourself what is good or bad. This flexibility in that judgment makes the concept of good and bad meaningless.

I mention this because the concept of good and bad gives us our justifications for our anger, disappointment, or despair. If you are a parent and your child is "acting bad," you might feel it is appropriate to be angry. You might try to convince yourself that you aren't angry with (or at) your child, but angry about the "bad" behavior. But what is the result? Does the child know you are angry? Do you punish them? If so, the child will learn that it's perfectly fine to get angry when someone disappoints you or does something you don't like.

While I'm saying that anger isn't good or bad, if our goals are spiritual freedom (and thereby freedom from *Fear*), having conscious contact with the God of our understanding, and being a conduit for unconditional *Love*, then anger is certainly a stumbling block. No matter how you slice it, anger is a manifestation of *Fear*, and *Fear* is just a word that describes the lack of *Love* moving in and through us. *Fear* will restrict the flow of *Love* or cut it off completely.

* * *

It is natural to get angry at things that offend us or make us afraid. Anger tells us something isn't right or isn't working the way we think it should. It's how we react to that anger and what we do with it that makes a fundamental difference in our spiritual health.

It helps to understand what anger is. As I mentioned earlier, anger is nothing more than an expression of *Fear*. *Fear* can result from fright, disappointment, assault, offense, injustice, jealousy, regret, and so on.

If we think someone is disrespecting us, the strength of our anger is directly proportional to our sense of self-importance.

"How dare you talk to me that way!"

"You embarrassed me in front of my friends!"

"Why won't you pay back what you borrowed? I need that money to pay my bills!"

"You broke your promise!"

"Hey! Don't cut me off in traffic!"

"You hurt my feelings."

"You cheated on me. How could you?"

"Those people are so nasty and mean to those other people."

This list goes on and on. What is the common thread,

though? ME. It's all about me. I get angry about what you did or didn't do for (or to) me. I get mad because you didn't do what I expected you to do. I get angry because someone doesn't behave like I think they should. I get mad because someone does something to someone I care about, and I internalize it and make it my own.

We get angry when we fear we will lose or have lost something we want or think we need. We get angry when we are possessive, afraid that person or thing will break away from us. We get angry when we are scared that we will lose control of something or someone—or if we have lost that control. We can be angry at others or even at ourselves. And when we become angry, we have judged someone or something to be unworthy of unconditional love.

Frequently, we get angry at people because they exhibit something that we dislike about ourselves. We see something reflected in their behavior or attitude that touches a sore spot in our minds, and our anger is a way to reject that truth and prevent that person from touching it again, although that rarely works. In these cases, we have to take action and get rid of our self-judgment.

Anger is also a cycle of *Fear* that will perpetuate itself. Anger is a burning poison in our minds that consumes so much energy. It takes the energy you need to be happy. It comes from a place of lovelessness, and then it blocks the flow of *Love* within us and keeps us from being recharged. Where does the energy come from, then? It has to come from somewhere, and if your energy source (*Love*) is cut off, you have to take it from somewhere or someone. So, you can take energy away from the things you enjoy doing or the things you need to do. You can also turn your anger on someone to get them angry, and then steal that energy from them. The reverse can be true, too; someone might provoke you to anger for no apparent reason, just to pull your energy in to feed their anger and fill the emptiness it has made inside them. It becomes a relentless cycle that can consume us and makes us miserable inside and out. Anger creates resentments that are toxic and destructive, like a cancer in the mind.

Have you ever been so angry that you couldn't think? Have you been so mad that you gave up on something you really wanted? Have you broken things or ended relationships because of your anger? And how do you feel while you are angry, and afterward? Pretty awful, right?

Anger needs to be dealt with the moment we feel it, before it fills us with poison that corrodes our joy and spills out onto others. We can start by asking questions of ourselves:

Why am I feeling this anger?

What's my part in this situation?

Why am I taking this situation personally?

What do I gain from being angry?

Is my anger a reflection of my own fear and self-doubt?

Am I jealous?

Am I angry because this situation makes me feel guilty about something?

Am I afraid that this person's behavior might expose my hidden feelings?

There are, of course, many other questions we can ask ourselves, but the point of these questions is to examine our thoughts deeply. As soon as anger stings us, we need to stop for a moment of self-reflection and find out why we are hurt.

It is difficult to avoid anger in the face of injustice, but we must evaluate whether our judgment is truthful. It might be that our own identity, our sense of self, is really what is being threatened. Should you be angry if someone walks up and punches you for no reason? Not really, but the initial fear and confusion will probably lead to a lot of anger if you let it.

The majority of our anger comes from some type of assault on our self-importance or ego. If, however, you practice the art of not taking anything personally, you will be a lot less likely to become angry if you are insulted or even assaulted. Whatever meanness or hatred someone directs at me is about them and whatever is happening in their hearts and minds. It's got nothing to do with me—unless I started it by directing my poison at them. Again, this is a time for some deep self-reflection.

Of all the things I can do to reduce the chances that I'll get angry at someone or something, refusing to take anything personally is at the top of the list. I already know I am important and wonderful; I don't need anyone to tell me that I am or am not. Whatever someone thinks of me isn't my business. We all have our own perspectives, and everything we perceive is tinted through the lens of our thoughts and experiences. That's true for everyone. If someone tells me I'm a terrible person, I have a choice of believing them or not.

The power belongs to you, not to the person who has tried to provoke you—unless you surrender your power to them. If someone tells me I'm horrible, that's only their opinion and has nothing to do with who and what I truly am. The same is true if someone tells me I'm awesome and great. It's their opinion, and that is something that they made up. I already know myself, my strengths and my weaknesses. I love myself without any condition or expectation, and I refuse to judge myself as good or bad. I am what I am. I am glad when I can spread *Love* and joy, and very thankful for the opportunity—but once I have released that energy, it's out of my hands, and it's no longer up to me how it is received, if at all.

When you love yourself unconditionally, you stop judging yourself, because judgment is based on conditions. When you refuse to judge yourself, it's unlikely that you will accept the judgment of others, because you know that whatever they are saying is a reflection of who and what they think they are. When you love yourself unconditionally, refuse to judge yourself or others, and don't take things personally, you gain the freedom to respect everyone's right to tell their story however they see fit. That kind of respect for others makes it very hard to be angry at them.

If you're mad at me for something I said or didn't say, or did or didn't do, who is responsible for the pain the anger is causing you? You, and only you. It's totally up to you to forgive that person or situation and refuse the anger and poison it brews.

What if I make a mistake and hurt someone accidentally, or even on purpose? Some days are better than others, and when I'm not at my best, I might make a mistake that causes someone pain. I might break something. I might damage a relationship. But if I have learned to stop judging, and how to love myself unconditionally and forgive myself, it's very easy to do my best to make amends and offer healing for their wounds and mine.

When our actions or inaction have made someone angry, we aren't afraid to apologize and ask for forgiveness if we're not embarrassed or ashamed. That means I've had to forgive myself before approaching the person. That way, I can make amends freely and honestly. I can also be prepared for them to reject my apology, and not take that personally, either.

Resentment

If I offered you a valuable, beautiful, comfortable-looking chair, would you take it? What if I threw in free delivery? When you got the chair in your home and positioned it just right, would you love the chair? When you sat in the chair, and it gave you a painful electric shock, would you stay in the chair? If you got shocked whenever you or anyone you love sat in the chair, would you keep the chair? If the next time you saw me, I offered you another chair, would you take that one, too?

Resentment is like this. It looks like something we ought to hold on to, but when we get close and touch it, it zaps us. What does it do to the person, thing, or situation we have resentment against? Nothing. Nothing at all.

* * *

If you've ever been in or spent time around anyone who's been in a twelve-step program, chances are you've heard the expression "Expectations are premeditated resentments." One of the many benefits of spiritual freedom is living without expectations and fear of judgment. We learn to stop judging ourselves and others. We love ourselves and others without any conditions or expectations. No one has to perform or behave a certain way for us, because we love them just the way they are and respect their ability to tell their own story any way they see fit.

Likewise, we tell the story of our lives in real time,

and we do it authentically. As we do, we respect and allow others to interpret what we show them however they see fit. We don't expect anyone to understand or receive our stories the way we want them to. If we did, we would change our story to fit our expectations of them, and we wouldn't be authentic.

Resentment is often defined as anger at being treated unfairly. Resentments can also be a much larger bucket that carries a variety of perceptions about many people, places, or things. Frequently, though, resentments stem from unrealistic expectations and an overblown sense of self-importance. Expectations that someone should treat me a specific way or do something that I want them to do— even if those demands are reasonable—can be a setup for resentment. The easiest way for me to avoid resentments in the first place is to reset my sense of self-importance, suspend my judgment, and accept other peoples' right to tell their stories how they see fit.

The world is a stage, and its people are merely players—but God help me when I think I can or should direct! As soon as I attempt to take on that role, all those empty resentment buckets line up for a refill. I've mistakenly convinced myself that I know how to direct your life better than you do. Besides being arrogant, it's also incredibly disrespectful.

Once resentment has formed, it needs to be dealt with directly. I have to acknowledge the resentment, and I need to make sure that I don't stir up any more anger or hurt in the process. I used to dread going through and deconstructing resentments. Today, I am grateful for them because I get an opportunity to practice and improve myself.

Finding the will and energy to forgive can be very hard when dealing with something particularly traumatic. It can cause a feedback loop where you might feel guilty or frustrated that you can't forgive. This is why self-love and self-respect are so important to this process. It's important to set out in the beginning not to judge your performance or ability to forgive something difficult—or anything at all, for that matter.

Even after years of practice, some resentments have taken me a long time to get through. Some things were so unfair and hurtful—things that were done ages ago that still have a tangible impact on my life today—and it is suffering through those consequences of someone else's actions, the sheer injustice of it, that pushes the pain and anger to the surface. With those powerful resentments, I need to take extra care and more time to process them. Not all resentments are created equal. Some are deeper, and some are harder to deal with; maybe they were just too painful, or the pain is still active right now. But with time, patience, and willingness, those resentments can be lifted.

The critical point for me is that whatever it was that caused the resentment in the first place was the active hurt; the resentment is the passive hurt that I carry with me. I can't change what happened, but I can remove that passive pain. Why should I continue to suffer? Why should I deny myself the true *Love* I deserve? Why should I surrender my joy because of something someone else did—or something I can't undo?

I've found that actual forgiveness isn't hard at all. It's building up the will to accept my life just as it is and to let go of the anger and frustration that I've grown used to.

Resentments are silent killers that don't just hurt you, but hurt those close to you. How? The energy that we burn on our anger gets used up. We can't use that burnt energy on the things that matter: living well and sharing love. Like that free chair that shocks you, resentments aren't worth hanging on to. Whenever you try to sit on one, it's just going to hurt you and the people you love and who love you.

* * *

You don't have to get ready to start cleaning the house. You just do it. Use the power of your intention, or your will, to start right now. Make a list of resentments that you've been carrying around. Resentments can be about people, places, things, or situations. You may resent a car wreck or a flood. You may resent injustice and bullying. You may resent someone who hurt someone you love. You may resent God. You might even resent yourself.

Make a list. It doesn't have to be perfect, because a personal spiritual inventory is a living list. Just get down the biggies. Once you start taking away the big stuff, the smaller things will be exposed, and you can deal with them, too. New hurts may also come along. Write those down, too. This process isn't about perfection; it's just progress.

Once you're satisfied with this inventory, take a moment to experience the emotions, but don't dwell on them—just a few seconds or a minute. Decide if you had an active part in what caused the resentment in the first place.

If you did, then you'll want to forgive yourself, too.

One by one, meditate or pray on each item on your list. Whether it's God, gods, or something else you can understand to be bigger than yourself—perhaps unconditional *Love*—ask that force to help you release the stranglehold you have on those hurts and resentments. Imagine what it would be like not to be angry, fearful, and hurt. Imagine that each item on that list is a piece of wood, and then imagine a fire in a fireplace. Put each one on the fire, and feel the warmth and energy that it emits. Just like a piece of wood in a fire, let it burn down to ashes in your mind. And just like the ashes, let it blow away in the wind.

Grief and Sorrow

Grief and sorrow fit in this chapter on *Fear* because of what sorrow does inside our minds. Sorrow, or sadness, is a manifestation of *Fear* that has been realized. However, it is active because we are afraid of what life means in the face of loss. Sorrow can be paralyzing, and grief may transform into regret, guilt, or even resentment.

When we are living in the moment, flowing with the abundance of the energy of *Love*, sorrow doesn't have much time or space to take root. It isn't that we no longer experience grief; we will. But instead of ruminating on sorrow, we quickly lean on our Faith and acceptance.

In this plane of existence, of space-time, there is a beginning and an end to every physical thing. That is an immutable rule of this universe. Of course, if we get metaphysical about it, we can say that there are no beginnings or ends, only transitions, and that would also be true. There is only one energy in the universe that takes many forms. Everything is energy transformed into light and matter. So, in that framework, the passing of one thing marks the eventual beginning of another.

That's fine on paper, but it looks a lot different when we lose someone close to us. It feels significantly different when someone we know leaves us (whether by death or departure) than when someone we don't know very well (or even at all) leaves us. Why is that? The simple answer is the attachment. I truly enjoyed my grandmother's company, her warmth, the sound of her laugh, and her spirit. Even though I knew it was coming, I was devastated when her body died. I wasn't spiritually awake back then, but I am sure I would ache just as much today. On the other hand, I don't think I would grieve the loss the same way, because my perspective has shifted very far from what I believed then.

There is no judgment of grief or sorrow here. It is what it is, and it will serve us one way or another. I miss the people who have gone away from me, but I am not sad. Instead, I am grateful for what I gained in being with them that allows me to feel any loss at all.

It's fine to feel sadness, sorrow, or grief. It's okay to grieve. These feelings remind us of what we appreciate in the world around us. However, suppose we dwell in grief and sorrow. In that case, we are vulnerable to losing touch with the moment and equally vulnerable to developing more harmful thoughts and emotions, such as anger or resentment.

We must all deal with our grief as it comes. Again, I don't think there is a right or wrong way to do it, and I imagine that every event that brings sorrow is unique to the person and the moment. But what if there was a way not to feel any pain in loss? I'm not saying that in and of itself, grief is bad. It's neither bad nor good, but the pain is pain, and emotional pain is always rooted in *Fear*.

* * *

There is a threshold in our spiritual progress, and

once it is crossed, the entire universe looks very different. Clarity of thought exists only through that door that doesn't translate well on the other side, so I hope I can do this justice. With that clarity comes the understanding that everything is as it is supposed to be. The situations of my physical being may not be what my mind wants or even needs, but the Knowledge gained within the fullness of spirit tells me that it doesn't matter. However real it may be to my body's senses, the physical world is just an illusion. Good and bad, right and wrong, joy and sorrow are the illusions that add texture to our physical experience.

What we truly are is eternal. We come from a place without space or time. There is no dimension to eternity. Everything that exists does so because it is eternal, but what we are experiencing now can only exist in this form. We may choose to have purpose and seek the connection with truth, with *Love*, and with each other and find harmony while in this form, or we may not. In the scope of the eternal, it doesn't matter. What does matter is whether or not we choose to enjoy this experience here and now.

We have something in this form that doesn't exist when our form is eternity. We have the experience of time. We have the experience of creativity. We have the experience of emotions. We have a sense of separation that gives us uniqueness, and we can use that uniqueness to experience this form with each other. This form is neither better nor worse than the eternal form; it's just different. At some point, our time will end, and whatever energy we are made of will merge back into the *Source* and exist as eternity, not as the physical and temporal beings that we know now. When eternity needs time, a new universe will explode into existence, and the process will start all over again. Our eternal being will spread out again into new life and new form.

When someone I have attached to dies or moves away, I am still left with an imprint of their energy. Psychologically, I have my attachments and the closeness we shared, and there will be an adjustment and probably a bit of pain. However, if I am firmly grounded in the *now*, my perception is much different, and I will see loss as an experience to enjoy rather than grieve. I understand and I know that person and I are both made up of the same energy, that we came from that same *Source* and that we are the *Source*. To think that I've lost something is to stick my head back into the illusion.

It would be easy to mistake detachment for coldness or callousness, or perhaps a defense mechanism. I'm sure it could be both, but there is another reason for it: attachment is a poor use of time and energy. I know I don't want anyone to grieve over me when my body dies. Will they? Perhaps, but I hope not. It won't bring me back, and it only pulls them away from the moment.

Psychologists might scold me, saying we need to grieve and process the loss. I would respectfully disagree. We don't need to experience emotional pain; we choose to. We do it because we want to or because it's expected of us. We do it because people will console or even pity us in our sorrow. It is a choice that is perfectly natural. It is how humans have been conditioned, that we must go through the emotional abyss.

As I said, there's nothing wrong at all with feeling sadness, grief, or sorrow. But if you are aware that you don't have to feel those emotions, they won't sting so much when you do.

Expectations

How does the subject of expectations fit in the context of a chapter on *Fear*? When we understand what expectations are and how they affect our thoughts and emotions, the connection to *Fear* becomes more evident.

What is an expectation, then? Most of us know what the word *expectation* means: it is a firm belief that something will happen in the future. Expectations take many forms. If I am in a position of authority and direct my charge to do something, I will expect that thing to be done. If I've ordered something online and paid for it, I expect it to be delivered to me when promised, or at least eventually.

There are also hidden expectations—things we don't often think about consciously or constantly, but which we still believe. Relationships with others come with expectations that are often unspoken. I may expect my friends or family to be loyal or supportive. I may expect my lover to be monogamous. I may expect marriage to improve my relationship. I may expect my children to be obedient.

In the previous section about resentments, I mentioned that expectations are premeditated resentments. This is because, generally, our expectations are tightly coupled to our egos. The relationship between expectation and *Fear* boils down to our fear of not being in control. It is also a fear of losing or not gaining what we desire. An expectation can symbolize our fear of not being acknowledged. In some ways, if our sense of self-importance is warped and ego-driven, our expectations may be created by our fear of being exposed and not as important as we want to be.

Even at the most superficial and benign level, expectations can be hazardous to our spiritual and emotional well-being. Take something as simple as expecting an outcome when preparing hard-boiled eggs. I will put water in a pot and eggs in the water, put the pot on a stove, and turn on a burner beneath the pot. I've made boiled eggs countless times before, and I know what the outcome of those events ought to be. After so many times, the expectation of the intended result is automatic. There is no wonderment or ambiguity to it. I follow the same steps as before, and after a few minutes, I have my hard-boiled eggs ... unless, of course, something unexpected happens. Maybe the stove doesn't work right, the power is out, or the pilot light went out.

If I've grown dependent on my expectation being fulfilled, I may get upset if I don't get my hard-boiled eggs when I expected to. Perhaps that was what I was planning to eat before leaving for work, and I had just enough time to prepare the eggs. Since something went wrong, I didn't get what I wanted, and I had to leave hungry. Then I'm disappointed that I didn't get my hard-boiled eggs for the rest of the day. I might even let this event put me in a bad mood—a mood that impacts the way I interact with people at work or at home.

Not getting the snack I wanted might be too trivial of an example. It's no big deal; it's happened before, and I came out fine. But what if the expectation is something much more important? A long time ago, there was a television show called *The People's Court with Judge Albert Wapner*. In one particular episode, a man had loaned his fiancée a significant sum of money. The relationship ended, but the woman never paid back the money, so the lender took his ex-fiancée to court. The judge asked many questions about whether there was a promissory note or anything in writing that would prove the money had changed hands and was a loan. There was none. So, though he seemed sympathetic, Judge Wapner said, "You know what you call a loan when the relationship is over? A gift."

The point of the story is that when the two were "in love" and planning to be married, the expectation that the money would be repaid was natural, strong, and probably automatic. What Judge Wapner said, in effect, was when the relationship changed, so did the expectation. If, however, we cling to that original expectation regardless, and it isn't fulfilled, the result is resentment.

In relationships, especially when we idealize them, we create expectations subconsciously. The reality of the relationship is skewed by our imagination—how we want it to be, and how we hope it will progress. Within those visions and hopes, our expectations grow. Often, in our minds, the other person in the relationship is more of an ideal than an individual. Even when we're unaware of them, our expectations will overshadow the true relationship and deny the other their right to tell their own story. When they don't behave the way we want them to, our expectations go unfulfilled and create fertile ground for resentment to grow.

As we get to know people, we usually adjust our

expectations to match what we experience rather than what we've fantasized about. But each time the other misses the mark and fails to meet our expectations (again, whether we're aware of them or not), a new crack forms in the relationship, where resentments spring up like weeds through broken pavement. If we were unaware of those expectations, we are likely to be unaware of the resentments festering in their place. It changes the filters through which we view that relationship and how we idealize it. Eventually, we give up and let nature take its course—or worse, end the relationship with lots of drama.

In my life, I have indeed been angry because someone didn't do what I expected of them. Whether it was a broken promise or someone not living up to the ideal I had of them, the expectation was replaced with resentment. But

the truth is that my expectations are about me, not anyone else. It isn't up to me how someone chooses to tell their story or live their life. It isn't up to me to dictate the standards that others live by. Even if I follow the Golden Rule and treat others as I want to be treated, that doesn't give me the right to expect others to treat me the same way I treat them. If I believe that the way I treat people is good, kind, and just, but then I expect the same treatment in return, I'm completely missing the point of being good, kind, and just. However, if I approach those around me with unconditional *Love*, that lack of conditions is the same as a lack of expectation.

Expectations are conditions. They are agreements with the people and things around us that we intend to be honored—even if we're the only person aware of that agreement. What I have found is that living a life without expectations is freeing and gives me the power to live authentically. I cannot possibly practice unconditional *Love* if I hold expectations, even if the expectation is that loving someone unconditionally will make me happier or make my life better somehow. If I love you unconditionally, I do so without expecting anything in return or expecting that I will benefit from it.

If I can love myself unconditionally, I can release the expectations of what that might mean and how that might make me feel. A long time ago, when I was first discovering the concepts I've been writing about in this book, I had great expectations. I expected that if I could follow the advice and tenets of those I perceived to be spiritual masters, then my life would change for the better, and I'd be able to live in bliss. Instead, my expectations turned into impatience, which morphed into disappointment and resentment. I resented myself for what I thought was failure. I resented the spiritual teachers for being unclear in their teachings or selling me a bill of goods. I resented the world around me for interfering in my quest for a better self.

To put it another way, I was afraid. I was afraid of being stuck in misery. I was afraid that I wouldn't find the peace I believed would help me. I was afraid of being permanently broken. Within those fears, and combined with a strong desire to just be happy, I created expectations of which I was hardly (if at all) aware. I read into the words on the back covers of the books I pored over, creating expectations based on what I mistook for promises. When those promises weren't fulfilled within a certain amount of time that I considered reasonable, I got angry.

I don't want to be misleading here; I wasn't angry or resentful aggressively. It was subtle and unnoticeable at times. Little things popped into my thoughts, such as discounting the wisdom of what I'd been reading or listening to, dismissing some spiritual teachers as opportunists. At times, I felt that the promises that I perceived—and let's be honest, some spiritual writers make big promises about how much their book will help you—were out of touch with reality or just out of my reach. I was angry at myself for being unable or unwilling to put those words of wisdom into practice. I judged myself harshly, and I despaired.

* * *

For obvious reasons, it's easier to dispel our conscious expectations than our subconscious ones. With some practice, we can learn to be loving and generous without expecting anything in return. We can learn to allow people to be who they are without expecting them to be how we want them to be. We can put our energy into things without being emotionally invested in the outcome.

Some expectations happen organically and may seem innocent or benign. For example, in relationships with loved ones, there is often an expectation of permanence. This is an expectation of desire, or what is often referred to as "taking things for granted." In the previous section about grief and sorrow, I said that the power and intensity of our suffering are directly proportional to our expectation of permanence. These expectations don't have to be rational or realistic (and they often aren't) to be powerful and intense.

So, how do we dispel these types of expectations? It isn't an easy thing to break away from subconscious expectations. They're usually automatic and a product of a lifetime of conditioning. I don't want to lose the people, relationships, or things I care for. It is that want, that desire, that creates the seed of expectation that can grow and flourish in the back of my mind. But I've also found that taking a regular personal inventory of what I value allows me to truly appreciate those things and not take them for granted. When I acknowledge my emotional connections to people, situations, or things, I can take that moment to acknowledge that nothing is permanent or guaranteed. I can then appreciate those things I cherish with a lot of gratitude. This doesn't automatically rid me of expectations, but I can release them a little at a time as I continue to practice.

* * *

You might think me silly or unrealistic when I say, "Do everything without expectation." Surely if I go to work, for instance, I ought to expect to be paid for my labor. Well, yes and no. Employment is an agreement. It is an exchange of labor or services for something else of value, usually money. Both parties expect to get what they're trading for in this agreement. That's reasonable. The danger is when we become emotionally invested in the outcome. If I have a contract or agreement for employment and I don't get paid, I can seek remedies to get what's owed. Of course, we could argue philosophically that the payment isn't truly an expectation if there is recourse for the failure of one party to fulfill their obligation. (That, I think, is splitting hairs.)

I think it's perfectly reasonable to expect to be paid

for my work, and be paid on time. By the same token, it's reasonable to understand that things can go wrong that cause that expectation to go unfulfilled. It could be an accident, an oversight, or malicious. There are lots of ways I can react to that unfulfilled expectation. Some ways are just business, and some ways are emotional and personal. It's the emotional and personal reactions that I want to avoid.

Not getting a paycheck on time (or at all) when I expect it can have serious repercussions that greatly impact my life. If, like most folks, I'm living paycheck to paycheck and don't have any savings to fall back on, bills and debts may go unpaid. Late fees, interest charges, collections, utility cutoffs, repossessions, evictions, and foreclosures may result from that missed paycheck. That's a lot of hurt and worry that will likely get created.

But what if I'm not emotionally invested in the outcome? Yes, life may get pretty hard, and I can lose a lot of stuff and even be forced to pay a lot more for things. It isn't fair; no doubt about it. However, suppose I can release the expectation that my life and livelihood will be as I'd hoped? In that case, the emotional trauma from such an adverse event is reduced or even eliminated. I don't have to surrender my serenity and happiness for hardship. It's my choice if I do.

By releasing the expectation that my life will roll along just as I like it, hardships become just a part of life, and not a reflection of the quality of my life. There is very little in this universe that I have any real control over. Permanence is an illusion. Things change whether I want them to or not. My health and the health of those I cherish are not assured.

I've got no control over the economy. I have no control over the weather. I have no control over world leaders.

I'm not trying to be bleak. My point is that there are a few very important things I am in control of that make all the difference: I control my thoughts, I control my desires, and I control my love and my connection to the *Source of Love*. The strength of my spiritual discipline doesn't matter nearly as much as my awareness that I have the choice to be happy, content, and blissful despite my circumstances. There is no reason why I cannot be joyful in poverty or wealth. And I can be just as happy with my freedom as I am in prison.

There is something of a trap that I fell into a long time ago: I conflated comfort with joy. In other words, I expected that if I were comfortable, I would also be joyful. That, unfortunately, is not entirely true, but I can still be joyful even when I'm not comfortable. It was far from easy for me to accept this truth, but it's always been true, whether I accepted it or not. Life is dynamic, and we are always in motion. The one constant in the universe is *change*. Thus, the one expectation we can have that is truly neutral and benign is that there will always be change.

* * *

The very first step in releasing harmful expectations is, of course, willingness. Just be willing to let go of the expectations that cause you and the people around you harm. Be willing to accept life as it happens. Be willing to be happy regardless of your level of comfort.

Releasing expectations takes us out of a place of *Fear* and into a place of wonder. I understand the probable outcomes of the things in which I invest my time and effort, but those outcomes are not always certain. Once I accept that, there's a bit of adventure to be had. I know that things may not work out the way I intended. In reality, I don't know what's going to happen tomorrow. I don't know what prosperity or hardship lies ahead of me. I am free to chain my happiness to outcomes, to expectations, but I am also free not to.

Expectations prevent me from living in the moment. They prevent me from being present here and now, because I have chained myself to them. Expectations constantly pull my attention toward an uncertain future and—even ever so slightly—force me to try to manipulate my circumstances to ensure the expectation is fulfilled. The more my attention is pulled out of the moment, the less attention and energy I have to be in and appreciate the only moment that exists: now.

I'm not sure if it's realistic to think that we can totally rid ourselves of all expectations all the time. I know it is possible, but that is an exceptional state of being, a way of living that is extraordinary and probably undesirable to almost all human beings. Everything in the universe must balance. Indeed, if we give up our expectations, we gain serenity. But to completely rid ourselves of expectations requires much more and brings us close to—or into—transcendence. Transcendence requires a lot more of us; it requires the complete surrender of self. I'll get into this in more detail in the chapter on enlightenment. For now, it's enough to know that we gain serenity, peace, and happiness for each expectation we release or refuse.

Empathy

Empathy is amazing. It helps us relate to others and understand more deeply what they are going through and how their feelings affect them. The true blessing of empathy is that it allows us to absorb the *Love* energy radiating from others (and from the universe itself). However, how we react to our empathy is important. The more powerful the empathy, the greater the need to guard against importing fear. I say "importing" because that's what we're doing when we feel empathy for someone: we're creating our own copy of what we believe they are feeling and how we believe we would feel if we were in the same circumstances.

Empathy in itself is not a problem, but absorbing the *Fear* of others can push our *Love* energy aside, or even block it. That seems counterintuitive; empathy is similar to compassion, and compassion is a form of love, as it evokes a desire to help relieve someone of their pain and distress. The problem is that the energy we absorb from others in the process evokes emotions that are not necessarily our own, and those emotions are often based in *Fear*.

Except for those who live with psychological disorders that inhibit empathy (primarily antisocial, borderline, and narcissistic personality disorders), practically everyone has some degree of empathy. Some people are natural empaths whose empathy is so strong and affects them so greatly that it is more like an ability than an emotional attribute. No matter the degree of empathy that we may generally have, or how much we have at any given moment, when the empathy we feel becomes potent, we may think that we can somehow take away the pain of others. Empaths are much more inclined to feel this way. But it doesn't often work like that. We may absorb the energy that people radiate when they are experiencing strong emotions, but we're only receiving that energy like a radio picks up a signal from a station. We aren't taking anything away from them; we're only receiving the broadcast. But if we react with our own emotions, we create a copy of what we perceive.

I am not at all saying that there is anything wrong with empathy. We have that attribute for a reason. It is useful and often helpful. It allows us to connect and send and receive our *Love* energy with others. It can build a connection with others and guide us to show compassion.

For better or for worse, I am an emotional empath. I have struggled mightily with its effects in the past, and it is still a challenge today. Still, the spirituality that I share with you now has given me greater strength to put my empathy into perspective and understand its power much better than I did before.

Empathy is built into us, and it is very much like our five physical senses. If my emotions are strong enough, or your empathy is strong enough, you can *sense* what I feel. However, empathy doesn't give us the feelings of others in context. Some powerful empaths can draw in the bigger picture and the associated emotions, but most of us just absorb the feeling. When we do, our brains go into overdrive, trying to build our own context for what we're suddenly feeling. We may recall times when we felt like that ourselves, and the circumstances that brought those emotions about. Sometimes this happens only on a subconscious level; other times, images from the past come back in full force, whether the event was painful or joyful.

When we take ownership of those empathic feelings, we superimpose them over our own experiences, which can cause us serious trouble. Particularly with the negative, painful emotions, we feel the *Fear* those emotions are caused by. That *Fear* pushes us away from our own *Love* and pulls our mental and emotional energy away from our center and our joy.

Because empathy is hardwired into the hearts and minds of humanity, I must assume that it has a purpose and is meant to help us. In that case, I accept it as good, but I also recognize that how I react to it may not be good for me. I cannot stop being empathetic, and I wouldn't want to if I could; I love the ability to connect with other people on that level. But I must do so cautiously. Those feelings will come, and when they do, I must treat them the same way I do the emotions I create in my own mind. I acknowledge them, respect them, and then let them go. I bring my focus back to my unconditional *Love*. I tend to the work of healing.

We mustn't take the feelings we receive from other people personally. That seems obvious because, after all, the emotions emanate from something that has happened to someone else. The mind and the ego do not make this distinction, though. They feel the emotion, and if it is hurtful, they react to the pain the same way they would if the emotion came from our own circumstances. That is why we can get so angry at someone who has hurt other people.

It may be something we have read or heard on the news. It can even be a character in a work of fiction. But as far as the mind is concerned, any emotion is *our* emotion; the source doesn't matter at all.

When I absorb emotions empathically, regardless of whether they are happy, sad, or fearful, I pause for a moment and then ask myself some questions: *Does this emotion belong to me? Is this going to increase my ability to transmit my* Love *back to them? Am I going to be able to absorb and take away their pain?* The answer to each of these is always "no." And if the emotions I'm receiving and absorbing are the positive, happy, and joyful kind, I must still ask myself another question: *Is this feeling increasing my joy, or am I just sharing in it?* I need to ask this question because I can get addicted to feeding off others' joyful emotions and become complacent in dealing with my spiritual health. Sharing in the joy of others is amazing and is something to be cherished, of course—just with a little caution.

Naturally, we absorb the emotions of those around us, or even those of imaginary characters in a story. It is important that we don't internalize and take ownership of those feelings. My emotions have taken me from hell to heaven and everywhere in between. The chances are good that I have felt the same emotions that others are experiencing at any given moment. I think it is reasonable to assume the same for you. I can know what those emotions feel like without having to feel them again. We can convert our empathy into sympathy and become available without having to be hurt. I don't need to put my hand into a fire to remember what it's like to get burned. Releasing my connection to others' emotions ensures that I remain an open channel for *Love*, and my usefulness and purpose increase with the power of the *Love* that is within and flowing through me.

Chapter Ten: *Judgment*

"If you judge people, you have no time to love them."

—*Mother Teresa*

The Judge

Our internal judge lives mainly in the subconscious mind. When the judge makes its decree, it sends it to the forefront of our minds as a thought. That thought may take the form of an emotion or a sensation. It may be in the form of words or images. The judge chooses the method that will have the most significant short-term or long-term effect.

In his book *The Four Agreements*, Don Miguel Ruiz flawlessly describes this judge that enforces our unconscious law. He says, "There is something in our minds that judges everybody and everything, including the weather, the dog, the cat—everything. The inner Judge uses what is in our Book of Law to judge everything we do and don't do, everything we think and don't think, and everything we feel and don't feel. Everything lives under the tyranny of this Judge."

Ruiz further describes the judge as a parasite—and the way to kill the parasite is to break all the old agreements that went into writing your Law. The judge isn't easily or directly accessible; it behaves like a separate parasitic entity. The judge's favorite food is fear, guilt, and regret. These powerful emotions nourish the judge and help it grow, but are entirely toxic to our minds and spirit.

Since I don't think I can say it better, I recommend reading, learning, and practicing *The Four Agreements,* which is a cornerstone of my spiritual foundation. Those principles greatly influence my knowledge, methods, and practices. Anyone familiar with them will easily spot their influence throughout this book. These new agreements are as follows: *be impeccable with your word; don't take anything personally; don't make assumptions; always do your best.*

The other kind of agreements Ruiz speaks of are the threads of ideas that make up the tapestry of our beliefs. One agreement might be, "Blondes have more fun," or "I'll never be good enough," or "Nobody could ever truly love me." Some agreements are relatively benign, like "I look good in red," and others can be devastatingly toxic, like "I'm not worthy of love." These agreements (or thoughts) are implanted in our minds from the outside. Maybe someone said mean things to us, and we agreed with them; we accepted the thought and made it our own. Those thoughts and ideas get carved into the stone tablets of our internal law. From then on, everything we say, do, see, hear, feel, or even dream is judged by that law.

Some laws in our minds might seem beneficial (or at least benign). I might believe that I am a good singer, so I feel free to sing in front of people—even if I'm not that good by some standards. I may have been told that I'm a good dancer, so I agreed and accepted that into my law. Now when I dance, I judge my dancing as excellent or even outstanding—no matter what anyone else thinks or how many toes I break! But that doesn't mean that judgments that seem to work in our favor or boost our self-esteem are beneficial. They may well make you feel good about yourself, but there are much better ways to accomplish that without the presence of an internal judge that will turn on you in an instant and without warning.

Suppose the judge convinced me to think my singing is excellent. So, I decide to go to a singing competition and try out. To the people judging my performance, my singing is horrible and cringe-worthy. I may trust them as experts, and suddenly I'm faced with a new thought that contradicts what I believed to be true. I agree with their criticism that I'm a horrible singer. The judge then jumps on this opportunity and adds to my disappointment with humiliation. Now I feel truly terrible. I'm embarrassed and want to hide from the world. I might even agree with my internal judge so much that I begin to hate myself.

However, without the judge, this scenario can play out quite differently, because it comes from my own heart and experience: I love to sing. I can carry a tune and stay on key. I know that my singing used to be pleasing to the ear, but that isn't so true anymore. My voice is raspier, and my range is limited. Does that stop me? Nope. I sing because I enjoy it—not to get praise or attention.

Now, some people sing off-key or flat, and they can't hear that. They listen to what their imagination plays back to them; in their minds, they genuinely sing beautifully. If I were tone-deaf—unable to recognize proper pitch—I'd easily mistake my flat singing for excellence. Then if I'm looking for outside approval, I will get in trouble with my inner judge.

Remember, the judge presides over everything we do, say, think, or feel. The judge will impact my work, relationships, goals, and even appearance. The judge may rule that I'm not worthy of the kind of partnership I hope for. It will tell me that I'm just not good enough and put forth any excuse that sounds reasonable to get me to keep agreeing with that judgment. It will bring up past mistakes and criticism. Even if I'm being abused, the judge will try to convict me and make me responsible for the abuse, convincing me that I deserve it.

I don't want to make the mistake of personifying the judge. It is parasitic, but it's also mindless. It is a part of our minds, but it has none of its own. The judge feeds off emotions, but it has no sense of self-preservation; it will gladly kill off its host and die with them, if given a chance. The judge is a technique the mind uses to reconcile what we want and feel with what we assume we ought to be and do. The judge floods our minds with comparisons (often contradictory), so that we measure ourselves against truly meaningless standards.

We are born without a judge feeding off our fear. But as soon as we come into this world, other people begin teaching and training us in how to be human. I don't know when humanity created this judge, but I assume it was around the time humans developed language. Once we were able to communicate emotions with our thoughts and ideas, we gained the ability to share our judgment, too. Of course, there are nonverbal ways to convey judgment, but words have a kind of magic. Words are a lot less ambiguous.

Almost everyone wants the best life for their

children. The outside world is filled with amazement, wonder, treasures, cruelty, and danger. Along with the basics of language and self-care, we teach our young to be mindful. That learning, though, builds a need for approval. From birth to death, we are all indoctrinated into a system of rewards and punishments. It's often not fair, but it is effective. And once the internal judge takes root, it becomes self-sustaining.

Our self-esteem becomes defined by the thoughts decreed by the judge. The judge must first approve of the way we treat ourselves and others. If we defy the judge, it will try and convict us later on—unless we change our thoughts. But despite a lifetime of conditioning and expectation, we don't need the judge to be happy or to survive. In fact, when we kick out or starve the judge and strip away its power over our thoughts, we open up to a new world full of kindness, love, joy, contentment, and peace.

⋆ ⋆ ⋆

One kind of judgment helps us stay alive: discernment. We use this type of judgment to assess the quality of something before we interact with it. It helps us make all kinds of choices and decisions. Selecting an apple at the supermarket may include using discernment to pick one that looks best and doesn't have any worms poking out of it. Likewise, we can judge the best route to take to work based on our needs and preferences. That kind of judgment is fine and necessary.

The other kind of judgment is much more personal and emotional. We judge people, places, and things all the time. We see something, filter it through our experiences and biases, and then make an emotional judgment about it. We judge the people we meet and the people we love. We give everyone and everything a grade, but not consistently. We even do this to ourselves.

When other people judge us, we listen, then consider whether we believe their judgment or not. Still, even when we reject someone's judgment, we may hang onto a seed of doubt and begin judging ourselves the same way later on.

As we grow from childhood to adulthood, we learn to trust and believe our inner judge. We begin comparing ourselves to the kids around us and those on TV or the internet. We learn how to judge a whole person based on very little information. We judge people based on gossip or assumptions.

We may have been taught to believe good things happen to good people and bad things happen to bad people. If we see something bad happen to someone, we may automatically judge them as being bad. We judge ourselves the same way. If something good happens to us, we may judge ourselves as being a good person, but when something bad happens to us, we may judge ourselves as bad.

The kind of judgment that doesn't help us is the kind that is constantly trying to redefine who we are. Thoughts that come from the inner judge tell us we aren't good enough or that we don't deserve to be respected. One day, the judge may let us believe we are wonderful, but if someone says something critical or mean, or if we make a mistake, the judge comes down on us hard, and we have to listen to a lot of thoughts that undermine our confidence and self-worth. Thoughts that come from the judge can be painful, so we try to avoid that judgment altogether. We may not try something we want to do because we're afraid we'll be embarrassed and the judge will torment us. We might lie to someone to avoid their judgment—only to be judged by ourselves for lying.

There is no justice with the inner judge. The judgments that come from our minds are often not even based on any facts or evidence. No matter what we do or say, at some point, the judge is going to get involved and send us thoughts to consider, regardless of their truth or effect.

Guilt

I make mistakes. Sometimes I say things that make someone feel bad. It's never my intention to hurt someone's feelings, but sometimes it happens. A long time ago, I would have felt guilty for that, and even if I were able to apologize and make amends right away, I'd still punish myself over and over afterward. I wouldn't forgive myself until I felt I'd served my penance. That was not a great way to live.

Now when I make mistakes, I feel the emotions and the remorse, acknowledge them, then forgive myself. I need to release the guilt. Guilt comes with all kinds of extra baggage, like fear and anger. Sometimes, we feel like our guilt is unjust, and then we transform that guilt into resentment. In other words, we might hurt someone in a way that we are ashamed of or embarrassed about, feel the sting of guilt, and then turn that guilt into resentment against the person we hurt in the first place. We might even go so far as to spin this into a cycle, where we feel even guiltier for developing resentment against someone we hurt and are now victimizing again—at least in our minds.

I know that when I've felt guilty in the past, I felt that I was selfish for forgiving myself—or that I didn't have the right to forgive myself at all. But that's not how forgiveness works. Because I choose to care about the feelings and well-being of others, if I do something that hurts them instead, I'm causing harm to both of us. I've hurt myself, too. That's what guilt is: a self-inflicted wound. But what if, instead, we simply forgave ourselves right away? That was hard for me at first, because it seemed unfair that I should not feel guilty for a long time if I'd hurt someone's feelings. I had done a bad thing, so it was only right that I be punished, even if only by myself. What good does that do, though? Is that supposed to be a deterrent from hurting someone again? Do I need that—or can I feel the remorse, acknowledge it, be determined to do better, and then get on with the work of healing?

You see, that's the thing: we need to get down to the work of healing as soon as we can, while the event is still fresh in our minds. Forgiveness from the other person only ultimately serves their healing. They need to forgive us so that they can heal. We need to forgive ourselves so that we can, too.

Holding onto guilt serves no good purpose. If you have the capacity to feel guilt in the first place, you have the capacity to learn from it immediately. Forgiving ourselves does no disservice or dishonor to the object of our guilt. In fact, self-forgiveness empowers us to make an honest and full amends when we need to. Sometimes, it's hard to see someone we resent forgive themselves. If we are holding onto that resentment, we want them to suffer as much as our resentment is causing us to suffer. That's just *Fear*, not *Love*. It doesn't do us any good.

If I step out of line, embarrass someone, have a bad attitude, or become impatient with someone, it hurts when I recognize that I've caused someone harm or discomfort. That's all I need to get right to the business of healing. It's important for the person I've harmed, too. Guilt is toxic and can splash out onto the person to whom we're trying to apologize. We could even subconsciously give that person permission to harbor resentment, which adds to the initial harm.

I'm beating this drum because it's so very important to learn to release guilt right away. It isn't useful beyond the first few moments. Guilt ultimately stems from our empathy, reflecting what we think are their hurt feelings. We don't like it, and consequently we feel remorse. That's good; that means we care about how others feel. Once we have acknowledged our mistakes, though, we have to move on.

I remember when I was still spiritually asleep—maybe even spiritually *ill*. I had hurt someone's feelings intentionally; I was mean and hateful. Later, after I'd suffered enough of my guilt, I tried to make amends. I asked for forgiveness, and they angrily refused. I acccpted that they had every right to be angry and didn't owe me forgiveness. We parted ways, and I continued feeling that guilt for years. I thought I needed their forgiveness so I could forgive myself.

Now I know that served no purpose whatsoever; I merely compounded my guilt by feeling guilty that I thought I deserved absolution! If I could go back and counsel my younger self, I would say, "The guilt you feel is the wound you inflicted on yourself when you hurt someone else. They have their own wound that needs to heal. Letting them know that you are sorry for what you said or did, that it wasn't their fault, and that they did nothing to deserve such bad treatment might help them heal that emotional wound—

or it might not. You aren't responsible for how anyone else responds to their emotional pain. You are, however, responsible for your own. It won't do them any good for you to carry guilt. It won't undo what's been done to constantly punish yourself for it, either. Hurting someone hurt you. Learn from that, and use that as motivation to find a path to happiness."

* * *

We sometimes have internal dialogues and monologues, or rehearse the conversations we plan to have and replay the ones we've had. We replay scenes from the past—not just as memories, but as little plays. One of my worst habits is recapitulating events from my past and imagining how things could have gone had I done or said something different.

Exploring memories isn't bad in and of itself. However, what we do with those memories can have a damaging effect on us, building strong walls between ourselves and our realization of communion with the *Source* and our rightful state of grace and joy. Recapitulation is perhaps the most effective method to punish ourselves for our past mistakes. The stronger the emotions embedded in those memories—often remorse or anger—the more frequently and vividly we replay them.

Evaluating mistakes is helpful when we do it to learn from them and understand the consequences. For example, we can recall an instance where we hurt someone with our actions. Looking at our part in that event, we can see what went wrong and decide to make amends (more about that later) when it's needed. However, reliving and dwelling on past mistakes serves no constructive purpose.

What Other People Think of You is None of Your Business

We were all brought up to give consideration to the opinions and judgments of others. We naturally want the approval of our elders and peers. We want people to like us and think about us kindly. Sometimes, though, things don't go that way. Sometimes people don't like us and even say mean things to us. Social media is a primary example of this mentality. If we are rewarded with praise, which boosts our ego, we keep doing whatever we were praised for. If we are criticized or humiliated, we might stop doing something we really enjoyed.

All of us have experienced the pain of someone's bad opinion of us. When that happens, the judge gets very excited and adds to the torment in our minds. We may then try to change ourselves to avoid risking that bad opinion again. It might even make us depressed or lead us to dislike ourselves.

But what is an opinion, anyway? It isn't the truth; it's only a perception. As we know, human perception isn't very accurate and is only loosely acquainted with reality. No matter what I say or do, if someone is around to witness it, they're going to form an opinion. They'll judge what they've seen in some way. Judgments about me are made from their assumptions, hopes, biases, and emotions within seconds of their experience of me. Before it even reaches their conscious mind, whatever I've said or done is filtered through their experience and biases. Their mind wants to build a fuller picture of me as a person.

Even if someone has known me for years, they don't live in my head or heart, and all they know is whatever I've chosen to show them. They see the actor playing the part, but they cannot possibly know everything that's going on inside me. So, whether it's someone I've just met or someone I've known all my life, whatever they think about me is whatever they've created in their mind. Based on what little they know about me, could the image of me someone creates be accurate? Maybe; maybe not. It definitely won't be a complete picture. I have a hard enough time creating an accurate picture of myself! How could anyone else do any better? They can't; it isn't possible.

* * *

If we can grasp the idea that the opinions we and everyone else have about each other are at best blurry snapshots that can change in our minds over time, we can grasp the idea that those opinions don't ultimately mean anything. It's nothing personal. If someone criticizes me, they are telling me something about themselves. They can't tell me anything about myself that is totally accurate or something I don't already know.

We're not just talking about negative, hurtful opinions here; the positive stuff and praise fall in the same category. It's none of my business if you think I'm awful or great. That's all about you and what's going on in your mind and your life at that moment. I know who I am, and I enjoy what I do. I love and respect myself without condition or judgment. I enjoy writing, and even if every person on the planet told me I was a lousy writer, I'd keep doing it. What I'm doing is about me and what I like to do, not about them. Of course, if I didn't think anyone would enjoy what I have to say, I'd be less inclined to go through the effort of publishing my work, but it wouldn't diminish my enjoyment of the process.

On the other hand, if this or any other book I wrote became a global sensation, and everyone loved it and praised me for it, it also wouldn't mean anything. I'm putting this out into the world so I can help at least one person—not get their opinion of me. The moment that I worry about the opinions of others, I pin my self-worth on their judgment, not on reality.

This idea is key to not taking anything personally, whether good, bad, or indifferent. What other people think about you isn't really about you. It's about an image they have created in your likeness. When we stop taking anything personally, we open ourselves up to *Love*. And as we come to understand that opinions are generally meaningless, we are less inclined to form them about or share them with others.

What people say or do to you and think about you is about their perceptions, and consequently about themselves. If you refuse to take things personally and you refuse to judge others, you quickly realize that it is easier to *Love* them unconditionally. When you *Love* someone without conditions or judgment, you automatically respect them and their ability to live their lives and tell their stories however they see fit.

When people judge you, they aren't experiencing the richness of *Love*. They think they know how you should live or how to be better than you, but they don't. If they are judging others, they are judging themselves, too, and they're unaware that they don't have to. That's okay, too, if that's how they choose to tell their story and play their part.

* * *

Of course, there are times when opinions do matter. We may need some feedback if we're doing a job to know whether we're doing the job well. If we're trying to improve a skill or a hobby, feedback can be helpful. As a personal example, this book was submitted to an editor who fixed my mistakes and helped me make it better. She told me what worked, what didn't, what was good, and what wasn't so great. Opinions and advice are valuable in helping us make course corrections along our journey and get more enjoyment out of what we like to do. The key is to not take such things personally.

Criticism and opinions have value until we take them personally. If we submit any part of our identity or self-worth to a critique, review, idea, or advice, we move into *Fear* territory and out of *Love*. It's easy to tell when you've taken something personally because you experience an emotional response, like disappointment, discouragement, or embarrassment. But criticism and opinions that come our way are ultimately neutral—neither good nor bad—and it's up to us whether that criticism is constructive. If we take it personally, then the criticism or praise becomes destructive.

Even a malicious insult could be constructive if we can find a grain of truth in it that helps us improve whatever we are doing. But regardless of the intent of the person directing their opinions at us, it is our responsibility to refuse to take them personally, and our obligation to accept or reject the value of those opinions.

No matter what, whether we ask for an opinion or not, what other people think about us or our work or the things we love says something about *them*. What they think is all about them and whatever image they might hold of us. If someone praises me and tells me that I am good, that doesn't make it so for me—only for them. On the other hand, if someone criticizes me and tells me I'm awful, that doesn't make it so, either. It's only what they think based on the very limited information they have. It's an opinion, not a fact. I'm not good or bad; I just am. I don't need anyone's judgment or opinion to tell me who I am or how satisfied I should be with my life.

This idea might take some getting used to, and a lot of practice. I worked this concept into my mind to address my feelings whenever I realized I was being reactive and taking something someone said personally. I reminded myself that taking things personally, even if it hurts, is just my ego trying to make me feel important. But I *am* important. So are you. So is everyone and everything. That's all any of us need to know: we are important.

Whenever I had those feelings because someone said something about my personality, I stopped for a second and asked myself some questions: *Is this feeling because I feel validated or invalidated? Do I need to be validated to feel good about who I am and what I do? Does this person know enough about me to even make that assessment? Why do I have to feel differently based on what they've said than I would feel if they'd said nothing at all?*

I admit that this was something of a challenge for me, but I've been doing this for so long now that it's become second nature. In the early days, though, it was hit-and-miss. I just kept trying, and I didn't get down on myself when I didn't do as good as I wanted to. It was hardest with praise. Who wants to turn down a good ego-stroking? The problem is that it's just as big of a trap as internalizing the negative stuff. I can take criticism and feedback and apply it if I want to, or I can shrug it off. Regardless, the thing that I need to watch out for is taking something from the outside and using it to define who I am on the inside.

It's Nothing Personal

If I can remind myself often that it's none of my business what anyone thinks of me, I can take back a lot of my personal power and use it where it serves me better.

I know there are times when people say or do things that work against me. Sometimes people are mean and abusive. That still isn't personal, even though it can cause me real harm. I have to deal with the consequences of someone else's actions sometimes, but that's part of the package of being human. Life can be made difficult by things that are avoidable.

It can be very difficult not to take something personally when there is a tangible effect, such as loss of life, limb, or property. Someone could express their opinion to someone else, and it might cost me my job. Something like that can cause a cascade of damage and hardship, and I'm left with a long-term daily reminder of the wrong done against me. Should I take that personally? It certainly seems personal. But it isn't. The impact of another person's words or actions may cause me real trouble, but the emotional component— my reaction—is completely my choice. It isn't personal at all.

Natural disasters and accidents happen all the time. Should I resent the river if a flood sweeps my home away and takes all my possessions? Should I feel like the river hates me? Should I define who I am by the way the river treated me? Of course not. I may not like living so close to the river anymore, but it wasn't personal. The river and the rain that swelled it are what they are and do what they do. The water isn't aware of me, my possessions, or my feelings.

It might be tempting to argue that neither the river nor the rain have brains, self-awareness, or morals. The water is unaware of its actions and unconcerned with the consequences. But a human being does have a brain, self-awareness, and morals. A human being is aware of the people around them and is concerned with consequences. That's true, and I agree that we should love and respect one another and make an effort to do no harm. However, the catch is a question of logic. If I didn't know who or what hurt me, would I still take it personally? That sounds silly, but it makes a lot of sense in practice. If someone has the capacity to be cruel and abusive, they'll hurt anyone; that's why it isn't personal.

The other side of that coin is that taking things personally submits our personal power to the actions and thoughts of another person. We build a world of assumptions to make sense of the surrendering of our personal power when we take things personally. We try to understand their reasoning, even if there is none. We wonder if we deserved the mistreatment. This creates a vicious cycle that drains more and more of our energy until we have little left to take care of ourselves.

The alternative is to understand that I am not responsible for the minds, thoughts, or actions of anyone other than myself. I don't control the people who praise me or tear me down. I have nothing to do with their decisions to behave the way that they do. It's nothing personal. I may get caught up in their flood, but the flood was never about me in the first place. With this knowledge, I can keep my personal power, and I can love the people who harm me the same as I do those who lift me up. I can live without judging anyone or contemplating their motivations. I can generate all the love I need, and then give the rest away. I can be immune to the toxins people sometimes feel the need to spread to the world around them. I can be happy no matter what circumstances I face, because my happiness is not dependent on anything outside of me, and because I choose to be.

Chapter Eleven: *Love*

"It is in this way that we must train ourselves: By liberation of the self through love, We will develop love, We will practice it, We will make it both a way and a basis, Take a stand upon it, store it up, and thoroughly set it going."

— *The Buddha*

Love Is

The word *love* conjures up many different images. There are many different kinds of love at the emotional level, too: romantic love, familial love, friendly love, pride, and fondness. I can love chocolate or a sunny day. I can love my pets. I can love my mother. I can love my sister. I can love my friends. I can love my spouse. Each of these things makes my body feel a certain way. There is joy in all these different relationships.

Since we can feel emotions physically, we may confuse certain feelings with others. Frequently, however, the feeling we call "love" isn't really love; it's desire or attachment, and it's conditional. We might fall in love with someone, only to fall out of love later on, because of betrayal or boredom. We may love a certain food, only to find it disgusting years later. We may love a pet, until it bites us.

Like spiritual *Love*, true emotional love comes without any strings attached. I think almost everyone understands, at least, what unconditional love feels like. If nothing else, we all long for love without judgment or fear. Authentic love occurs organically. The feeling is warm and comforting in the chest. Thinking about such love instills a sense of peace.

The *Love* that I've been writing about is beyond something dependent on the mind. It is not just an energetic force; it is the *Source* of everything. *Love* is eternity activated into this universe and everything in it. Stars, planets, earth, water, air, fire, rocks, trees, animals, and people—everything is made up of energy and light, and that energy is *Love*.

When I write about this energy, I always capitalize and italicize the word *Love*. I want to set this word apart from emotional love. I use other words to describe the same thing—God, the *Source*, eternity—but it's all the same. So many other spiritual teachers and I use the word *Love*, because when we connect our mind to that spiritual source, we feel it in our bodies and emotions much like human love. The clearer our minds, the stronger the connection, and the stronger the connection, the more potent the feeling. It brings peace, joy, and even ecstasy.

Love gives us energy that we cannot get from anywhere else. If we are not aligned and connected with *Love*, we must pull our energy from our reserves or take it from someone or something else. *Love* heals our minds and bodies in ways that science is aware of but can't quite explain. The simple reason is that it is the *Source* of life and all things.

Love can be nothing but unconditional. It can't be possessed or hoarded. It cannot be altered in any way. *Love* is. It can't be quantified. In spiritual *Love*, everything is the same because everything is equally valuable. Because *Love* is eternal, there is no beginning or end. It is limitless. It is impossible to express that energy in degrees. It's either flowing, or it isn't. *Love* can't be qualified. There is no greater or lesser quality of *Love*; it just exists and is perfectly pure.

* * *

Everything in this book is about plugging into the *Source* and allowing *Love* to flow through you. That is our natural state. It is how everything was before the world was corrupted by blocking the flow of *Love* with *Fear*. It may seem strange that the early humans would choose to build hell around them instead of staying within the joy and bliss of *Love*, but I think they wanted to see what it was like to feel separated from the *Source* and then get trapped in *Fear*. They forgot who they were and lost the ability to tell their children who they really were. But some of the stories remained, because not all of the humans got lost.

The energy of *Love* exists regardless of our awareness of it. Just like the codes in our DNA, that energy is hardwired. The memory of it exists in stories, but also in itself. There is an essence of *Love* within us. Often called the spirit or soul, that essence cannot be disconnected from the *Source*, but we can be completely oblivious to it. That's why becoming aware of it is called "spiritual awareness," "awakening," or "conscious contact." We don't tap into something that exists "over there." We only clear away the debris and disbelief that buries and obscures what we truly are.

Our beliefs generate thoughts that distract us, tell us

what's real and what isn't, and flat-out lie to us. Our thoughts tell us that if we can't sense something, it doesn't really exist. We live in an illusion that isn't real, but which we can't seem to disconnect from. Ironically, though the illusion isn't real, anything can be real in the illusion.

You might wonder why *Love* would ever do something that would cause it to feel disconnected from itself. There is a perfectly good reason, but it's hard to understand when our heads are buried in the illusion.

The intent (or will) of *Love* is to expand. *Love* doesn't exist in eternity; it *is* eternity. Eternity is nothing like what we know. We are physically bound in space-time. We experience moments and sequences and the passage of time. We perceive matter, space, and distance. If I say, "We have a long way to go, and it will take a long time to get there," you understand linear time and space. We have dimensions in our universe.

None of that can exist as *eternity*. Only intent exists. When *Love* grows, it creates a moment that cannot exist eternally. The only way that *Love* can become active is to create something that allows for that, and a universe is born. Here we have the tools needed to complete the expansion of *Love*.

By its very nature, *Love* must be free. So, when *Love* expands, that "new" part must be allowed to choose. It's a binary question: "Will you love me?" To answer any question, the options must be considered. What does the "yes" or "no" look like? The illusion of the world was constructed so that we may fully explore the "no."

For many of us, though, we feel compelled to explore the "yes." Unfortunately, humans have been strengthening and perpetuating the illusion for thousands of years. It isn't malicious. It can't be judged as bad or good. The illusion is merely a tool, like a hammer, that can be used to build or destroy. Honestly, it doesn't even matter how we got to this point. What is important is that something inside us senses the vibrational energy of *Love,* and we want to move toward it.

I think of it as hearing a music box playing the most beautiful song from somewhere in a messy room. All these clothes and things are piled up all over the floor. I can hear the music, but I'm not sure where the sound is coming from. Is it under that pile? Is it in a drawer, the closet, or under the bed? And how did that music box get in here in the first place? I didn't know I had one! Where is that thing?

If I want to get to the source of the music, I will have to do some cleaning up. I need to get everything in order and put it away. There is too much stuff piled up, and every time I try to push some of it aside to get to the music, another pile collapses and covers it up again. Our mind is the messy room, and our thoughts are like those piles of stuff scattered all around. Every time we try to push thoughts away so we can find the source of the sound, more thoughts come tumbling in.

The bulkiest thoughts that fall and hide the sound of *Love* that is calling to us are the ones that say something bad will happen to us if we break free of the illusion. We have a fear of the unknown. We've been saddled with some kind of fear or another our whole lives. We think that is natural, and any other way is too foreign to comprehend. I promise you, it isn't! You can live without fear, anxiety, anger, and guilt. You can live as joyfully as you want. You only need to listen to the music and carefully put away the thoughts that have hidden it all along.

Fearlessness

To live in *Love* is to live fearlessly. All the things that cause us pain cannot take hold of us when we have the power of *Love* flowing through us. All the feelings and emotions we call "negative" are rooted in a lack of *Love*. But when we are filled with *Love*, there is no lack, so there is no *Fear* or all the little fears it provokes. The result is fearlessness. That doesn't mean you can't get scared or nervous; you just won't be controlled by *Fear*.

It can be difficult to break any habit, and reacting to *Fear* is one habit we are all experts in. It comes naturally to us because that's the way we've believed things are supposed to be. But when we channel *Love*, we are acting instead of reacting. We are the light that dispels the darkness of *Fear*. The more we practice, the more we see that the things that used to cause us to be afraid or angry are either unimportant or don't even exist. We are able to pull wisdom from the *Source* and see this world for the beautiful work of art that it truly is. All those things that we thought were impossible become effortless. "Love your enemy as yourself" becomes a natural extension of our being. We no longer despair over suffering or injustice, since we know it's just part of the illusion.

* * *

To live fearlessly means that we have quieted the thoughts that used to bring us pain and sorrow. We've tamed the mind into accepting itself and the body as a vessel for God to experience this moment. There are times when the mind rebels and tries to deny the truth, but we've practiced, and we can calm our thoughts and give ourselves comfort.

At the beginning of our awakening, the mind desperately wants to return to the familiarity of the illusion. It's psychological that we tend to gravitate toward the familiar, even if we're fairly certain it isn't good for us. Deep down, the mind is less afraid of the fear it's familiar with than the unknown. The process of taming the mind starts with gently rejecting the thoughts that cause us pain. We address thoughts that deny our excellence and perfection, and then we refuse them any further attention. The mind will then rebel against something new and send us thoughts laced with the fear of failure. It may compel us to give up and return to the way we've always lived. We learn to quiet those thoughts that try to discourage us from living without *Fear*. We are gentle with ourselves and slowly convince our minds that it's going to be a lot more fun to live fearlessly.

Living in the illusion of the world will always throw challenges our way. Some will tempt us to go back to our old ways and pull us back into *Fear*. That's why we always practice and do those things that improve and maintain our conscious contact with *Love*. If we do fall into old patterns, we already know the way out.

Living fearlessly is a side effect of living in *Love*. It's the natural way to be and feel as *Love* flows through and radiates from us. Fearlessness and *Love* are attractive to others who can faintly hear the sweet music of the *Source*. Because we are unafraid, we are present and available to share that light and *Love* with anyone and everyone. Our presence then stirs the sleepy souls that long to be awake with us.

Respect

Along with natural and automatic forgiveness, *Love* also begets respect. When we *Love* unconditionally, there is no judgment. There is no desire to judge the way others tell their stories. Instead, we respect them and their choices. If someone we know or meet is stuck in the illusion and living in *Fear*, that's for them to do.

We respect that everyone can find their way to wherever they choose to go. In the full light of *Love*, we can see that everyone and everything is just another iteration of ourselves trying life out differently. If I know that you are really just me with a different mind and body, I must respect your decisions because they are also my decisions.

In this life, I've chosen to connect my mind with my spirit and enjoy the bliss that comes with conscious contact with God. Sometimes, though, I choose to feel the emotions of *Fear*. I might get anxious or angry. I might allow my mind to drift off into worries about the future or recapitulate the past. But I respect myself, and I let that play out on its own. I know where my true home is. The same can easily be true for anyone else. The best that I can do is be present in the moment and available should anyone need me.

Sometimes when we break a cycle of addiction (the illusion of the world is very addictive), we subsequently judge the behavior of the people around us. If we see some reflection of what we were like just a little while ago, we might judge that person. We might even tell them there's a better way to live. However, that is disrespectful; we're saying we know how to run their lives better than they do. Like you and me, everyone has the right to live their lives and tell their story the way they choose to.

It's very tempting when we see someone stuck in a situation like the one we were stuck in to want to give them a hand. We may think that we're doing them a favor by showing them the way out of the darkness. But in doing so, we are making some assumptions about that person. First, we assume that they want what we have. We also assume that what we have is better for them than their current situation. In addition, we assume that they aren't capable of finding their own way. In any case, we are making judgments, and if we act on those judgments, we're reacting to *Fear*, not acting out of *Love*.

Helping others find their inner peace and happiness is often what we want to do. When we are awake and aware, we are in a great place to help others. What we need to understand, though, is that some people don't want help. Even though we now know there is a more peaceful way to be, some people prefer drama and fear. Indeed, some people don't know they need help until it's too late. Not everyone can be brought out of the illusion. In fact, most of the people on earth at this moment will never know that they are asleep and dreaming a dream of *Fear*.

When we *Love* people unconditionally, their condition doesn't matter at all. The *Love* we have to offer doesn't come out of our humanity; it comes from our divinity. We are available, or we make ourselves available. Our presence is often the thing that is needed to truly help others.

Chapter Twelve: *Forgiveness*

"Forgiveness does not mean ignoring what has been done or putting a false label on an evil act. It means, rather, that the evil act no longer remains as a barrier to the relationship. Forgiveness is a catalyst creating the atmosphere necessary for a fresh start and a new beginning."
— *Martin Luther King Jr.,* A Gift of Love

Forgiveness is the Ultimate Expression of Love

WHAT FORGIVENESS ISN'T

I was recently asked a question that I found remarkably commonplace. The question was "Someone did a very horrible thing to me. Will God forgive me if I can't forgive them? Will I go to hell?"

The biblical answer to that question is fairly complicated, and the answer will vary depending on the doctrine in question. But ultimately, it doesn't matter what God thinks or does; if you cannot forgive someone for hurting you (even horribly), you're already in hell. It cannot be stressed enough: forgiving someone is for you, not them. This is a fundamental misunderstanding of forgiveness and what it's supposed to do for us.

What if you don't forgive the person who caused you so much pain, and why are you already in hell? There isn't a one-size-fits-all answer, but I will try to break this down.

The first question I have for you is "What do you think forgiveness is?"

The answer I've often received is that the injured person doesn't want to let the perpetrator off the hook. They don't want to excuse or justify that person's actions. There seems to be some misconception that forgiveness is the same as condoning the act. It isn't, and it shouldn't.

The next question I have is "What does it do to a person if we refuse to forgive them?"

The most honest answer I've ever gotten to that question is "Nothing. I just prefer to hate them." Hating someone or refusing to forgive them is a form of rejection. Our mind tricks us into thinking there is power in it, but it's just the opposite. You can forgive someone and still dislike them, too. Neither hating nor forgiving someone does anything to or for them.

Of course, there can be a dynamic where the perpetrator will twist the idea of forgiveness into an opportunity to get close enough to hurt their victim again. They might see forgiveness as approval or permission. I think that the *idea* of forgiveness being the same as approval is a big fear held by many people who have been hurt by someone close to them, especially when they are still in contact with the person, be it a family member, a teacher, or a member of the clergy. One big reason people may not want to forgive is that they don't want it to happen again. But the person you forgive doesn't have to understand what forgiveness is or even know that you forgive them. Forgiving someone does not mean that they can now be trusted. It doesn't mean that they are allowed to hurt you or anyone else again.

What about when the person who needs to forgive and the one to be forgiven are the same person? "I could never forgive myself for what I did." There is no difference between this stance and refusing to forgive someone else.

Another question I'm apt to ask people is "What do you think you gain from holding on to this hurt?"

The thing about refusing to forgive someone in order to hurt them back is that it often appears to work. I might be able to perpetuate their guilt if I tell them I will never forgive them. That might bring me some satisfaction, but it ultimately won't bring me peace. The judge in my mind might be accusing me of being stubborn or mean. All I'm doing is pretending that I have some control or power over this person—that I have something they want, and I'm not going to give it to them. That might be satisfying, until they have a spiritual awakening, forgive themselves, forgive you, and begin to love unconditionally. If they learn to stop taking things personally, that false power over them disappears, and you're stuck alone with your pain.

When we refuse to forgive or convince ourselves that forgiveness is impossible, we're doing active damage to ourselves. Every time the thought of that person comes up, we have to relive the entire trauma so that we can reevaluate it and justify our anger and resentment. We have to feel the pain entirely over and over again. They might live in the same home as we do, or we may never have to see them again; either way, the actions we won't forgive will be repeated in our minds in a never-ending loop. If we must have some contact with that person, our inability to forgive gives our power to them. You are stuck as a victim in that loop. Someone adept at victimizing others can pick up on that and use it to their advantage.

When you forgive someone, you reclaim all your power from them.

What you must understand is that real forgiveness is rooted in real *Love*—unconditional *Love*. Forgiveness comes from that energy source and moves through you. When you forgive, you begin to wash away the poison created by your anger and hatred. You start to heal those wounds. With that *Love* comes self-respect and self-care. You build up a defense against lovelessness. You will be immune to their poison. They will no longer be able to poke at your wounds.

If I had to deal with someone whom I must forgive but who is untrustworthy, I might say, "I don't hate you, I love you—but I don't trust you, and I don't have to trust you. Whatever you might feel about that is your business. Forgiveness doesn't mean there aren't consequences; it just means I'm not going to hang onto the pain." I don't have to do that, however.

It might be a gift to someone to forgive them so that they can move on and forgive themselves. If I think that might be the case, I'm going to have a conversation with them and tell them the truth: they don't need my forgiveness. They need their own, and I'll let them know how to get it.

Forgiving someone doesn't usually change their lives, any more than resenting them does. We often think that the person we forgive needs to be grateful for that gift. But that is just a lie. Forgiving someone isn't for them; it's for ourselves. We can easily carry resentment against someone we will never see again. What good is it to that person whether we forgive them or not? We may have the chance to tell someone that we forgive them, only to have that person suggest we go do something physically impossible with ourselves.

I'm not suggesting that we don't tell someone that we have forgiven them; there are certainly people who would benefit from hearing it. It just isn't my problem if that person wants it or not. If that person doesn't love, respect, and forgive themselves, whatever I offer will be temporary relief at best. (This gets into relationships, and I hope to cover that topic in depth in a future episode.)

Forgiving someone abusive or unrepentant can be tricky. But that kind of forgiveness does not mean we keep accepting abuse. We accept them as sick people and reclaim our power and energy to spend as we wish. I've learned that it is within my power to walk away from caustic people and toxic relationships. I don't do drama. I can't fix anybody, and that's not what I'm on this planet to do anyway. No matter how deeply I'm committed to my spiritual health, I can still get my feelings hurt or be provoked into anger. But there isn't anyone on this planet who is so dependent on my presence for their survival that I need to take abuse to sustain them. An exception would be someone who had an illness that made them say mean things, but that person is indeed sick, and it's easy to understand that whatever they're saying is nonsense anyway.

* * *

There are three main components to forgiveness:

- Unconditional *Love*
- Acceptance
- Willingness

LOVE

Resentments mainly get their power from conditions and expectations that weren't met, as well as from fear and self-importance, among other things. On the other hand, the unconditional nature of *Love* strips away the excuses that glue resentments to our minds.

When we begin to love ourselves unconditionally, we naturally let go of the need for self-importance. We just know that we're important, without any need to prove it to ourselves or anyone else. Once we fill up our own tank, that same unconditional love spills out, and we look at everyone else through that same lens.

ACCEPTANCE

Acceptance is a hallmark of unconditional *Love*. Acceptance is the suspension of judgment, to the effect that forgiveness is no longer necessary. If I love you without conditions, I accept you as you are. Acceptance can occur outside of unconditional *Love*, but it is always present where there is *Love*.

Some acceptance comes with quiet resignation. If there is something that we don't like but know we can't change, we can accept that as the way things are. In that case, acceptance is the point where we stop fighting. This isn't the same as forgiveness, but there are similarities. Let's take same-sex marriage as an example. Many people were (and still are) against it, but when the courts in some countries ruled that it would be legal, some of the people who rallied against it stopped fighting and accepted same-sex marriage as a reality.

When we talk about the forgiveness that comes from unconditional *Love*, the acceptance that we feel is solid. It isn't based on the inability to change something; it's based on respect. If there are no conditions to our *Love* and our forgiveness is true, then there is no reason that acceptance would not materialize organically.

Suppose you have a family member whose behavior you had to forgive. You've connected to *Love* and have become spiritually awakened and aware. Although you have learned how to love unconditionally, and thereby you can forgive that family member for the behavior that offended you, they have not changed, nor will they change. If they are obnoxious and rude and treat you with contempt every time they see you, you don't have to forgive them all over again, because you've accepted them as they are and respect their ability to tell their story. It's important that you don't take their behavior personally. That way, you are not offended or annoyed; you are calm and happy.

Acceptance is an important ingredient in not taking things personally. We accept that people are the way they choose to be. Their thoughts, behaviors, and opinions belong to and are all about them. Likewise, we accept ourselves the way we are in this *moment*—not as we were and not as we think we could be, but as we are right now. We accept that we are as we choose to be. With all that acceptance, it's easy to not take things personally and to accept others as they are, not how we wish them to be.

Acceptance means we forego judgment. We accept the agreement that everything around us is just as it should be. That doesn't mean things can't or shouldn't be changed for the better; it just means that whatever we walk into is just the way it's supposed to be in that *moment*.

Every living being has the right to tell its own story in whatever way it needs to. We all do this, whether we're conscious of it or not. When we take advantage of love and forgiveness, then accepting people, things, and situations just as they are becomes second nature.

Acceptance can take quite a bit of practice. I've had to slow down and consider my emotions as they arise on my journey. I've learned to notice the moment I become uncomfortable with the appearance of someone or something. That's often the first indication that I'm consciously judging someone and writing their story in my mind. I can catch myself when I'm evaluating someone instead of listening to them. When I catch myself doing this, I'm often thinking of what I will say to them before they've even finished talking, rather than really listening to them.

We all have limitations of one kind or another. Our best on one day isn't the same on the next. I might be sick or need rest. I might be in a mood or dealing with a swing in my mood disorder. I may be disappointed or sad. I may be joyous and spiritually high. I may be preoccupied with something. These are simple things that can limit my ability to perform consistently from one day to the next.

I may not have the skill or knowledge to complete a task or answer a question. For example, I'm a computer person; I work in information technology as a web programmer. I can do all kinds of fancy things with code, but I'm not much of a graphic artist, and what I think looks good usually doesn't look so hot to others. I can build PCs, but I'm not an expert in computer engineering. Sometimes I make things look easy, or I appear a lot more capable than I am. That can set up certain expectations about my abilities and performance. But those expectations aren't reality, they're just an image someone else sees and has recorded in their mind. That image is based on their perceptions of me and a hundred other things as they understand them. I may make some computer-related tasks look easy, and that might create the impression that I'm an all-around genius with computers, but that isn't true. It really can't be.

The main takeaway here is that we have to be super careful with the images we create of people. Those images are based on a lot of limited bits of information. A lot of that information is formed from just a glance or a word, and we take that tidbit of info and write a huge story around it, filling in all the gaps to flesh out the entire person. How much of that image can actually be true?

Then there are the masks we wear. The roles we

play may be inaccurate. We might "flex" and try to impress someone. We might build up an expectation for someone else and then not be able to deliver. That's why we need to be authentic and as honest as we dare to be about ourselves. In *The Four Agreements*, Don Miguel Ruiz calls this an agreement to "be impeccable with your word."

The only expectation I can genuinely have for someone is that they'll be human and whoever they want to be. I may want to share love and joy with them and help make their day a little brighter, but it's not up to me if they're willing or able to accept such things. I sure shouldn't be disappointed or resentful if they aren't. If I love them and respect them, I offer what I can without expecting anything in return. Honestly, that's not always easy to do, but it is most of the time. Ultimately, acceptance just means knowing that people will be who they want to be and not how we want them to be.

WILLINGNESS

Willingness comes from intent. The intent is the trigger of your power. Your will isn't what you want or wish for; it's what you will do. We all have an amount of personal energy or power that we use to accomplish things in our daily lives, whether physical, mental, or spiritual. Without intent—without willingness—nothing gets done.

We load that energy up with intent, and we expend that energy with action. It's like a boulder at the top of a hill. The boulder is the energy stored up and waiting for intent. The push that sends the boulder rolling down the hill is the intent. Willingness also accepts responsibility for what happens when the boulder rolls forward, knocking down everything in its path. Willingness is the movement of the rock, the earth loosened beneath it, the grass and trees knocked down by it, and the place where it rests when it stops moving. All of that is intent. All the unknowns that happen are the intent. Even the consequences I didn't expect or didn't want are that intent.

Nothing happens without intent. Forgiveness cannot happen without intent. *Love* cannot flow through or from us without willingness.

When we're talking about forgiveness, we need to focus our intent carefully. We need to consider what we're about to send our energy out to do. We forgive people, places, and things so that we can heal. We heal so that we can grow in our spiritual love. We grow in our spiritual love to be happy and helpful, and to have purpose. The willingness needs to come with the understanding that every action has a consequence, good, bad, or neutral. Once we use our intent, the boulder is out of our hands.

Forgiveness is powerful. I'm not saying that we need to make a big plan to forgive and heal all our resentments at once; I'm saying we need to be thorough and accept that it is a process. Resentments are a poison, and if nurtured and allowed to build up, they expand and become more powerful. Like a surgeon cutting out a tumor, it's essential to get all of it so that it doesn't come back. It will come back if we leave even a little bit of that poison in our minds. Forgiveness has to be complete, and we need to be willing to confront as much of that resentment as possible to get rid of it and heal from the damage it has caused.

Forgiving for Tomorrow

When we eliminate judgment from our thought-life and live in the light of *Love*, we have already forgiven what is yet to come. If the *Love* I share is unconditional, nothing you say or do can alter or diminish that *Love* in any way. *Love* itself cannot be resentful or afraid, so it likewise cannot judge. If *Love* cannot judge, it can never reach a state where forgiveness becomes necessary.

Perhaps this is like the chicken or the egg: which came first? That question is much easier and simpler to answer when we're thinking about *Love*. *Love* just is. It cannot be assaulted or hurt. If a pine cone falls on a boulder, should the boulder withhold its love of the pine tree? Should the boulder be resentful of the pine cone? Of course not! The boulder cannot be injured, even when the elements and time wear it down into sand and dust. The boulder, the tree, and the tree's offspring all live in perfect love and harmony.

* * *

Forgiving in advance isn't something you actively do; it results from practicing unconditional *Love*, suspending judgment, and forgoing expectations. The only expectation we have is that our forgiveness of others is automatic and unconditional, just like our *Love*.

It has been said that misery loves company. The world around us is full of wounded people who can't yet conceive of a life lived in unconditional *Love*. Some may be hurt and angry. Some may be cruel and get their enjoyment from hurting other people.

There is something I have noticed during my spiritual journey that I've found challenging to deal with at times. A few people have felt the need to test the sincerity of my happiness and *Love*. I understood what was happening from a psychological perspective, but that understanding didn't make those interactions any more comfortable. The objective of the testing was to see if I was being genuine. If I wasn't, then their cynicism would be confirmed. But if I was steadfast, then there was a glimmer of hope that they, too, might enjoy a life of serenity. This is very important to keep in mind: people are always watching. They may not be watching you or me all the time, but if we spend enough time in the company of others, someone will be paying attention. This is why we should strive to always do our best and be authentic as much as we possibly can. When we stumble, we need to be ready to forgive ourselves instantly, move on, and continue to improve.

I've found that a good way to forgive in advance is to simply not take anything personally, maintaining the awareness that everyone has a right to tell their own story and that what someone says or does is not because of me, but reflects their own thoughts. If someone lashes out at me for something I've said or done, regardless of my intention, I owe it to myself to listen to the words, but also the message. If I've said or done something carelessly, I can be grateful for the feedback, regardless of how it is delivered. Even if someone is saying mean things, the words aren't as important as the feelings. In most circumstances, an apology does me no harm. At the same time, I don't need to be angry about or hurt by cruel or aggressive words, name-calling, or accusations.

Suppose I'm in line at the bank, waiting my turn. I get distracted by my thoughts and bump into someone accidentally. That person, though, has been having a bad day and is already upset about the circumstances in their life. Though I apologize for bumping into them, they react angrily and say something like, "Watch where you're going, idiot!" Of course, it's easy for me to sit here writing and think of what I might say. There is a chance that anything I say will be taken as an offense. Even saying nothing at all might be taken as an offense. I have no way of knowing, but I also have no control over that person's thoughts and reactions. I do, however, have control over my own.

If I am in the zone of practicing and radiating unconditional *Love*, my actions and reactions should reflect that. The anger or aggression inside someone that compels them to hurl insults has nothing to do with me. Insults are just words someone uses to express how they are feeling inside. Why should I feel bad if someone calls me an idiot? I know I'm not an idiot—and even if I were, that doesn't define who I am as a person, only my intellectual abilities. I don't need to try and internalize the words. In fact, if I don't take anything personally, an insult means the same to me as a compliment. They are just words that the speaker uses to express something about how they feel inside.

Meeting aggression with *Love* is more like being a sponge than a shield. Shields block and deflect, but a sponge absorbs. The insults and rudeness I absorb dissipate in the presence of my *Love* and don't get reflected back. This usually helps to defuse or de-escalate tense situations.

Occasionally, though, someone may approach me to purposely draw me into conflict. Their goal is to make me angry, and if I don't get angry, they will be disappointed and try again—harder than the first attempt. Sometimes people have emotional or mental problems that limit their self-control. Sometimes we might get punched in the nose for no reason other than the aggressor's own issues. As I go through these scenarios, I am reminded that forgiveness does not mean helplessness, and it doesn't mean we shouldn't defend ourselves from harm. Forgiveness is just an active expression of unconditional *Love*. It means that I'm not going to judge that person, but instead love them for no other reason than that they exist.

Forgiveness runs counter to the way the world has trained us to react. Our natural emotional defense is to hold a grudge—a resentment—against people who have hurt us, so that we don't let them hurt us again. We are trained to believe that withholding forgiveness will somehow punish the other person. Sometimes it even appears to work like that. But that is an illusion. Resentment only hurts the person who holds it. Resentments cost valuable energy to maintain and are never worth the price.

* * *

There may be people in our lives who are habitual offenders. Sometimes a person suffers from addiction or a mood disorder. They may be chronically ill or prone to behavioral issues. Sometimes adolescents can have behavioral problems related to their growth, hormones, or social issues like peer pressure. We learn to expect that sooner or later, someone will say or do something that will be offensive in some way. However, if we really do love them unconditionally, then we accept them just as they are, regardless of the storms that follow them. This, then, is another way that we forgive in advance.

* * *

I've illustrated this concept with other people in mind, but there are times when we can cause offense to ourselves. I live with a mood disorder, and my best can vary wildly from day to day. I am therefore prepared to forgive myself when I fall short. Counterintuitively, this relieves the pressure and helps make my best better.

If we are committed to living a life filled with and radiating unconditional *Love*, and we practice ridding our minds of judgments and expectations, forgiving in advance is simply a passive byproduct of those efforts.

Making Amends

Sometimes, we're the ones who need to seek forgiveness. Actually, we might be able to give someone an opportunity to forgive. Making amends, though, isn't so much about seeking forgiveness as it is an attempt to repair the damage we caused, without causing more, and give others an opportunity to heal. Sometimes part of making amends is just keeping my mouth shut and letting the other person unload all the poison I gave them, with interest.

Making amends starts with making new choices and living the amends in real time. When it comes time to communicate and clean up my mess, I have to get rid of any expectations of how it will go or what any of us will get out of it. I need to just let it happen, without hoping for a particular outcome. If I can't do that, it may be best to just stay away until I can.

There are some people to whom I can't make amends personally. Either they've passed on, I don't know where they are, or the hurt I caused was so great that any interaction with me would do more harm than good. While this is certainly far from ideal, it is good motivation to check myself before I say or do something that will need amends in the first place. But in those cases where I can't directly make amends, living my amends is the next best thing I can do.

* * *

Making amends is a bit more than an apology, though an apology may be all that's needed. Above all else, we have to consider how our attempt at making amends will affect that person. Sometimes, the best thing we can do to make amends is to stay away; our presence may only trigger painful emotions or stir up resentment. If there is any doubt, it's good to talk it over with someone you trust and to pray or meditate before taking action.

In twelve-step programs, members are encouraged to make a list of everyone they have ever harmed. It's a hard list to make, because you have to think about all the harm you've caused, which often comes with a lot of guilt. It's very important that we forgive ourselves throughout the process of making amends. Even if we don't create a list, when we have caused someone pain, we need to be able to forgive ourselves as honestly and completely as we are able before we can go to that person.

Guilt can be a strong motivator to apologize, and we might seek forgiveness so that we can release ourselves from guilt. But that's just being selfish and dishonest. It's like when someone gets caught doing something bad and is suddenly sorry for what they've done, yet had they gotten away with what they've done, they wouldn't be sorry at all. They say they're sorry for the act, but they are really just sorry they got caught. When we ask someone to forgive us just so that we can feel better, we're not truly sorry for what we've done to them, but for how it made us feel.

That is why we need to clean up our own side of the street before we go and try to clean up the mess we made on the other. You have permission to forgive yourself. If you feel guilty, then you have already felt the pain. That's enough justification for forgiving yourself. Though you hurt someone else, you hurt yourself in the process, and that ought to be forgiven. You are forgivable.

When we are sure that we are honest and our purpose is to benefit the person we've harmed, we can go to them and offer our amends. But we need to be ready and willing to accept whatever reaction we get from the person we're trying to make amends to. This is a good place for unconditional *Love* to be practiced. We should respect them and let them tell their story and tell us their feelings, no matter how it is intended. Most of the time, the person we apologize to is accepting and grateful that we've owned up to our mistake and made an effort to put things right. Other times, though, they may still feel hurt, angry, or resentful. They may lash out and let us have it. That's okay. It's not about us deserving the abuse as payback; it's about us loving and respecting another human being and accepting them no matter what they say or do.

The good news is that the more we practice being authentic and connecting with and being a conduit for unconditional *Love,* the less we have to make amends for.

Part Three

Chapter Thirteen: *Escaping Hell*

"If there were in the world today any
large number of people who desired their
own happiness more than they desired
the unhappiness of others, we could have
paradise in a few years."
— Bertrand Russell

Hell on Earth

If we define *hell* as a place of suffering and separation from God, then there is hell on earth. The illusion would make us believe that we are somehow separate from the *Source*, from *Love*, and that God is something outside and above ourselves—or that He doesn't exist. Even Jesus Christ was accused, tried, and executed for blasphemy by admitting that he was the son of God.

Even if we aren't aware of it, we are *Love*. We are made of the stuff. Our spirit joins our mind and body to it, and our minds and bodies are made of the same energy that is *Love*. We couldn't be separated from it if we wanted to, but we can pretend we're not and ignore what we are. That's the thing that keeps the illusion alive and on full power: people don't know or won't believe who and what they are. They live in *Fear*, full of anxiety, anger, and resentment, and they only delight in the little joys that break up the negativity. When we discover the truth and learn that joy and happiness are meant to be enjoyed full-time, the old way of living becomes unthinkable.

While we pretend to be separate from the *Source*, we easily accept that suffering is inevitable. We are made to believe that fear, anger, resentment, jealousy, and despair are normal. We are told to deal with those things the best we can and try to be happy.

Spiritually Free

After my spiritual awakening, I pored over all the books I could find—anything that I thought would help me progress along my journey and identify the route. The catalyst for all this was the truly desperate situation I was in. The reality I was facing was a nightmare, and I could find no way out.

A common theme within most of the self-help, New Age, spiritual, and Eastern thought texts I read is that this world is just an illusion. Nothing we see is real. That suited me just fine, because I didn't want my situation to be authentic. I'd made some truly awful mistakes and bad decisions that resulted in my situation, and it didn't seem that I would escape accountability. So, I skewed the words that I read to favor my hope—the hope that by some magic of will and intent, I could alter the reality around me and escape the consequences of the choices I'd made before becoming spiritually awake. Bear in mind that I was an infant as far as spiritual maturity is concerned. My thoughts and thought patterns were still evolving, and I still saw through the lens of the illusion I was trying to escape from.

I didn't quite grasp the concept of what it means to say that this world isn't real or that it is an illusion. I was thinking more along the lines of *The Matrix* movies from the 1990s. The illusion was some kind of construct created by some force beyond the control of the world's inhabitants. I suppose that would be a fair comparison, but the fictional idea in *The Matrix* implies that there is a way to extricate the self from the illusion into an awareness of truth.

As time went by and I tried to accept my situation, I still held onto a bit of denial. I fantasized about altering this unreality and manipulating it into something more palatable. Unfortunately, this misconception only impaired my growth and kept me tied to the illusion.

To be clear, I'm speaking of the Law of Attraction and manifesting through intent. In somewhat simplistic terms, the Law of Attraction and the concept of manifesting through intent are roughly the same thing. The idea is that you attract or manifest what you want through positive thoughts and intention. For instance, you might wish to have a car that isn't breaking down all the time. So, you set your intention and see yourself with a vehicle that works. Or you may be looking for something less tangible, like a promotion at work, so you set your intention on being in that situation, and you imagine yourself in that role. Through the power of your spiritual oneness, you attract those objects, situations, or relationships to you.

I misunderstood—terribly. The books about attracting and manifesting tend to be on the same shelf in the bookstore as books on spirituality and spiritual awakening, and they are often written by the same people. I just made the mistake of lumping one thing in with the other.

The most notable books that come to mind are *Think and Grow Rich* (1937) by Napoleon Hill, and *The Power of Positive Thinking* (1952) by Norman Vincent Peale. I'd already read those books long before spirituality was something I even thought I wanted, so when I got around to modern works on manifesting and attracting, I was somewhat familiar with the concepts.

I've found that I wasn't alone in my confusion. Quite often, when people seek spirituality, they seek peace and relief from their desperate situations. Spirituality offers comfort from the pain, and manifestation offers to change their external situation. These two things are not mutually exclusive and easily go hand in hand.

But what if the situation is inescapable—like being an actual prisoner? Can you genuinely manifest an open door or an escape? That isn't very likely or realistic. Instead, manifesting can open your eyes and mind to the opportunities that actually exist or present themselves. A calm, quiet mind—free from desperation—and a spirit full of the intent of *Love* will enable better deliberation, allowing us to make choices and decisions that are more in line with what we're after.

This is the part I want to address. Being in harmony with and a conduit for *Love* does not erase the consequences of whatever situation we're in; it just brings peaceful acceptance. The situation doesn't matter, because we are no longer defined by any situation, whether good, bad, or neutral. It's accepting life on life's terms, and whatever is going on is mainly detached from who or what we are. Spiritual freedom begets mental freedom from the pain and suffering we've experienced and seen around us. It enables us to care and love dispassionately, without judgment or reservation. It is peaceful and joyous, despite whatever suffering exists around us.

Manifesting and attracting things does work, and it works best with a calm mind. However, I can't entirely agree with the idea that stuff just materializes or is pulled to us magically. Instead, what is happening is that when our intent is well focused, and our mind is calm and accepting, we are much more likely to see opportunities that can be taken to move toward our goal. We're not standing still waiting for things to happen; we're moving toward our goal with extreme clarity of thought. When we believe that the thing we desire is attainable, and we then imagine ourselves with that thing or in that situation, we can imagine what we would feel like with that thing or in that situation. In that way, we recognize the elements of our environment or circumstances that match up with those thoughts, and we seize those opportunities and make informed decisions to achieve the goal.

For myself, I tried to become spiritually adept while also trying to "manifest" myself out of a terrible situation. All that did was put a massive block between me and acceptance. This may not apply to you, but I want you to be on guard and have clear and realistic expectations of what conscious spiritual awareness does and does not do.

* * *

The illusion is that we are separated from God, *Love*, and the *Source*. We are not and we can never be separate, any more than silence can be divided or separated from itself. We always have been and ever shall be the *Source*. We are just having an experience in time while we are in these bodies, which we cannot separate our *Self* from until this purpose has been fulfilled.

The illusion of separation creates real pain in the mind and body and manifests the feeling and pain of being separated from the *Source*. Because the mind and body are part of the illusion's construct, the false reality is reinforced, and we take it at face value. That's why being stuck in the illusion is often referred to as a "waking nightmare."

The rule is that we cannot remove the body from this construct. It is physical, just as the construct is. There are physical laws that make the whole thing work and appear the way it does. Some rules are rigid; some are more flexible. I do not doubt that miracles can be manifested through intent. How that happens, though, is beyond the scope of this book. Suffice it to say that if the universe and everything within it is created of *Love*, and our minds and bodies are vessels of *Love*'s spiritual intent, we are naturally imbued with that same creative energy. While this is fascinating to contemplate and study, it doesn't matter as long as we continue to forget our true nature and perpetuate the illusion.

I want to clarify why I even brought up the idea of attraction and manifestation in this discussion. We are all on our own path, though we are often parallel to each other at some point or another. Our paths diverge and come back together with the spirits of other people. Some things are alike that we will likely experience as we move around in this playground. My warning is this: misusing our power can be a setup for a fall from grace. To prevent this, if we channel our energies into so-called attraction and manifestation, we must do so without becoming attached to the outcome. We must do so without expectations of success or failure.

That last bit may be a paradox. How can you set a goal without expecting success? How can you apply your positive thoughts to imagining yourself with that thing or in that situation without expecting that you'll have it in the future? That question answers itself. I didn't understand manifesting until I abandoned the thought of it. Expectation isn't part of the equation when you truly follow the principles of attraction.

Let's go back to the example of the intent to attract a car that runs well. I don't just see myself with the car; I am convinced that I already have it. It is a suspension of disbelief. Is the car yet in my driveway? No, not yet—but that doesn't matter. Am I pretending? Yes, to a point—but it's more than that. The thoughts are not of a goal to be attained, but of a dream already realized—past tense.

To explain this in precise detail would take another (and much longer) book. It does "work," and even if we aren't spiritually awake or don't even intend to be, it draws on the way that the construct of this universe is made. There is no real mystery or magic about it, because it is natural. What matters is what you're using the power for. Is it to satisfy the mind-body, or is the intent to improve our conscious contact with God?

There is a saying in twelve-step programs that is meant to help beginners: "Fake it 'til you make it." This isn't a suggestion to be inauthentic; it's intended to get the person to try to feel what it's like to be free from addiction. It's the same idea as wearing a smile even when you're sad. In essence, the advice to "fake it 'til you make it" suggests manifesting freedom from addiction. It's a bit crude, but it does work sometimes. That suggestion could be followed up with "Imagine who you are and what you are like as a person free from addiction. How does that make you feel? Then embrace that feeling *now*, and cultivate it with what you get out of your program."

In the context of spiritual growth and development, there is a place for attracting and manifesting something in particular: set your intent and focus on your conscious contact with *Love*/God/the *Source*/your higher power. Imagine how you feel and what you are like within that connection and consciousness. How do you behave? How do you feel with a quiet mind? How do you interact with others when you are feeling peaceful and blissful?

Take this image and refine it over time. This is a journey, and progress is all there is. Do not compare yourself to anyone else. It's easy to admire someone who we believe has attained a "higher" consciousness, but we cannot know what is really going on inside them. Their relationship with the eternal is unique and personal. So is yours. You are already perfect, just as you are. Take that perfection into your mind and focus your intent on what you want your relationship with God to be. Embrace and embody that in your mind and your actions. Spiritual perfection is not something to be attained, because you are already perfect! What we are doing, then, is trying to remember our perfection and rebuild our conscious contact with creation itself.

In this way, we can manifest that awareness, and whatever time passes in this dimension will be filled with joy. It makes the journey that much more fun. As the saying goes, "Be the change you wish to see in the world." The corrections to our thought processes, the meditations, and the prayers we use to maintain our spiritual health—these things change and evolve no matter what the state of our consciousness might be. Even Jesus and the Buddha were capable of learning new things. Our journey never ends; it simply transforms. When the universe has fulfilled its purpose and contracts back into nothingness, our journey will begin anew, and another universe will erupt into being. While our consciousness will evaporate and be reabsorbed into *Love*, our intent and purpose continue on and on.

* * *

This brings me back around to expectations. As I've mentioned a few times, expectations are premeditated resentments. My spiritual progress was stalled until I learned to let go of expectations. Expectations are just projections of a future that may or may not materialize. It isn't easy to be in the now when I have set expectations. It is impossible to love unconditionally if I set the condition of expecting anything in return. My chances of attaining true unity with the *Source* are severely limited if I expect that anything I do will give me something I want—even in the most selfless way. I can only trust that by living in the light of *Love* and being a bearer of that light, the impact I make on the world will be in line with the intent of God Himself.

* * *

Now, you might wonder what could be left to do after reaching Nirvana, the fullest potential of spiritual awareness. I've asked that myself, and it occurred to me that this is the chance of a lifetime, but it's also a chance *at* a lifetime. This experience is unique and utterly foreign to the eternal being. Here we have time, and we have an adventure. We have agency where we can express love in a completely new and amazing way, but it is a way that is impossible within the context of eternity.

This life is our chance to play with a form of existence that has time and space. Because of our physical construction, we have thoughts and ideas. We have goals and accomplishments. We have relationships with other bodies. We have experiences. Of course, I don't want to paint eternity as a boring place (it isn't a "place" anyway). Boredom requires thoughts, feelings, and time; none of that exists eternally. Nothing exists in eternity, yet eternity exists, and it exists only as *Love* and intent. If we could feel what that's like with our emotional minds and bodies, it would be bliss beyond all imagining. I believe that some essence has been retained in our collective memory, and thus we describe the afterlife as heaven.

To feel heaven, though, we need something to feel it with. We need the mind and body we are born with to connect to the spirit, enabling us to feel the effects of the eternal with blissful and peaceful joy and emotion. This is what we were made for and how we were made to be. The story of humanity's fall from grace and getting kicked out of the Garden of Eden represents how our ancestors forgot what they were. Since then, we have suppressed that memory and exchanged it for an illusion of a world separate from truth, from *Love*, and from God.

There have undoubtedly been people born into awareness who lived in their bodies and yet were completely oblivious to the illusion around them. They could see everything through their spiritual eyes from birth to death. People like this still walk among us now. For them, the chaos played out by the things in this world is silly, but they know that we are all free to play and imagine this realm however we see fit. I suspect that those beings born into their fullness of spirit have no idea that most people are trapped in the illusion like a fly in a spider's web.

I say this because there comes a point when our conscious contact with our true self, with the *Source*, overtakes the perspective we once had, and we begin to see the world (and all creation) through a completely different lens. We don't forget about our humanity or what it was like when we were stuck in the illusion, but we don't judge it, and we don't continue to recapitulate the pain we felt when we thought we were separated from God. The illusion is what it is, and it came about organically. It isn't bad, and it isn't good; it just is. There just isn't any further need to participate in or perpetuate the illusion, nor do we make any judgment about the illusion or those who still believe in it.

Chapter Fourteen: *Into Practice*

"Change your thoughts and you
change your world."
— Norman Vincent Peale

Breaking Free

Over and over, I have related my idea of the purpose of life. I say that *Love* must expand, and *Love* must be free. When *Love* grows, it asks the new part, "Will you love me?" This creates a moment that cannot exist in eternity, so a space-time universe has been designed to accommodate the pause between the question and the answer. While it may seem odd that it has taken 13.8 billion years to get this far, and the question is yet unanswered, for the eternal *Source*, time means nothing, so billions of years go entirely unnoticed.

While I have spoken in the abstract where *Love* asks itself, "Will you love me?", this doesn't happen in isolation or eternity. It happens right now. Understand that now is a constant. It is the thread of time itself. Now is a point in space where time flows through in one direction. For now, there is no past or future.

The bodies we have, these vessels for our eternal spirit selves, are temporal. Whether or not we know it, we are always in the now. Our minds and egos perceive this differently and create constructs for history and a future yet to come. Even though my brain is physically fixed to the now, it is never content with the present. It's always trying to be a time machine, constantly traveling between the past and the future, only pausing in the present to see what's changed.

If we are going to tame the mind, we need to convince it that our spiritual self, *Love*, is our natural state of being. We need to train our thoughts to love and respect this moment. We can accept that the mind's perceptions are always delayed, and everything we can perceive of the world's illusion has already passed. Only the spirit within our minds and bodies can be fully aware of the now. It isn't bound by perception or realization. It just is.

There are a few things we can do to tame our minds. First, we need to love our brains, minds, and bodies just as they are. We must forgive our human nature and commit to no longer judging our thoughts and actions. We need to trust that the spirit within us is wise and will guide our thoughts and behavior in a way that will bring love and joy to everything and everyone around us—even those who might refuse to accept it or who are in too much pain to be able to receive it. We must also forgive ourselves for our past mistakes. This cuts the rope to the past that pulls us away from the now. Likewise, we must surrender our expectations in order to cut the rope that draws us into an unrealized future.

Of all the things we can do to awaken our spirit, loving ourselves and others is the most important. Without this, we cannot forgive, and we cannot stop judging. When I first began my journey, I thought loving unconditionally would be the hardest thing of all. I was wrong; it is the easiest thing to do, because that is the true nature of our being.

In the chapter called "Love," I wrote about a technique I use to help myself and others imagine and feel what it is like to love ourselves unconditionally, without judgment or expectations. Once we convince our minds that this can be done, we must commit to it and practice it all the time. We know when we are not practicing unconditional *Love* because we feel the effects of *Fear* creeping in. When that happens, we stop for a moment, focus our attention and will on ourselves, and recommit to love. We forgive any thoughts, actions, words, or emotions that might have caused any harm. We start fresh, again, without judgment or expectation.

A new and wonderful connection came to me while I was writing this. It was so obvious, but somehow I'd missed it! This thought brought me so much joy, and I have to share it with you now. The metaphor I use to describe the purpose of our being is that we, as spirits, are here to answer the *Source*'s question, "Will you love me?" We know that the *Source* must love us because the *Source* is *Love*. It's just a matter of us answering back. I've always imagined this as something abstract—that my answer comes in the form of my awakening and awareness. Of course I love you! And I felt it deep in my soul, but I realized there was something else I could do every single day.

I am the *Source*. It isn't something apart or away from my true self. It is me. That is true for you, too. You are the

Source! That is your natural state of being. So then, there is something we can do using our ego minds to reinforce this. Look in the mirror and stare deeply into your own eyes. If you cannot see or cannot see very well, feel your body, touch your face if you can, and say your name out loud two or three times. Say your name firmly one more time, thinking of yourself with love, and ask, "Will you love me?" Think about that question for a moment. Ask it again: "Will you love me?" Feel the force and power of *Love* flow through you. "Will you love me?"

Now, if you're ready, answer the question with all the love of your being: "Yes! Yes, I love you!"

Let's Make a Deal

I have observed some resistance to giving ourselves over to *Love* in myself and others. At first, I couldn't quite understand it. What could be so wrong with living in the light of *Love* and a state of grace? Rationally, I understood how this could only benefit my well-being in almost every aspect of my life—mind, body, and spirit. Why, then, would I or anyone else resist this?

It comes down to trust. Until we become aware of the power we receive when connected to the *Source*, our ego is ignorant that there is a different way to live. Up to the point where we finally surrender and accept our rightful place within *Love*, the ego has been doing all the heavy lifting and directing every footstep.

As I progressed along my journey, I tried to love others without condition or expecting anything in return. After all, I had all the *Love* I'd ever need flowing through me from the *Source* itself. Coupled with expressing unconditional love to myself and others, I had to strip the judge of its power. Guilt, regret, resentment, and anger are only manifestations of *Fear*, and *Fear* is but the absence of *Love*.

I wasn't quite ready for a real fight inside my mind early on. The more I practiced loving and forgiving, the closer I felt to God and the better I felt mentally. Still, there was something in my mind that resisted this change. As I pondered this, I began to have those all-too-familiar dialogues—the back-and-forth internal conversation that often results in bad decision making—but I think they were helpful in this case. The methods and ideas I relied on to get me started on my journey created an adversarial relationship between different parts of my mind and personality. I needed to change how I thought and felt, because I was miserable and dying. I knew there had to be a better way than whatever I'd been doing. I thought about the facets of the personality and the mind that I'd learned about in college. The way I was going about spiritual growth only reinforced my internal conflict.

It was my intent—my will—up against a lifetime of habits and personality development. With a spiritual awakening to push and pull me forward, I was ready to do whatever I could to cement the change I needed to continue my growth and realize my potential. The saving grace was that I knew and understood the importance of self-love and self-respect. I also began to embrace self-forgiveness.

Have you ever had someone tell you that they forgive you, and you had no idea what they were forgiving you for? If not, will you imagine that for a moment? You see, that's what I'd done to myself! I started by telling myself that I forgave all the harm I'd done to myself and that I was ready to forgive anything in the future. For one thing, I only have the one brain, the one mind, and the one ego, but I was treating my ego like it wasn't a part of me. I was trying to be emotionally detached from myself. I don't want to suggest that there was anything particularly wrong with my approach; it is necessary to forgive ourselves and forgive the messes our minds often get us into. I just didn't consider that there is a way to go about this that could be a little bit gentler.

What I was doing was judging myself—my ego—to justify the need for forgiveness. My intentions were good and honest, but I tried to pretend that one part of my mind was better than the other, which created a bit of feedback. What I might have done was to start with the idea that forgiveness need not imply guilt. Forgiveness is just an expression of unconditional love, and it can go unspoken. I only needed to give love to myself to understand that forgiveness is automatic.

* * *

Our minds can complicate things, but they aren't that complicated—or at least, they are predictable. Diving into new and unexplored experiences often comes with some measure of fear or nervousness—in other words, resistance. The resistance comes from our mind's struggle with the unfamiliar and the inability to make predictions. When we consciously decide to move our thoughts and focus onto something esoteric like the power of *Love*, the mind can't form an image or compare it to anything. The proposition I make in this book is that we quiet our thoughts by calmly acknowledging them and refusing the ones that won't serve us. We can meditate and practice finding the gap between the thoughts, then widening it until fewer and fewer thoughts bombard us each day. That is not what the mind is used to. Its primary function is to think, and it has been throwing as many thoughts around as possible.

I hope it's easier for you, but I had to convince my

mind (myself) that it was going to be okay with this new way of thinking and being. At times, it was like I was talking to a child that was afraid to go to a new school: "It's okay. You'll be safe. You'll have fun and learn new things." Ultimately, I made a deal with my mind: I gave myself permission to jump right back to the "old way" at the first sign of danger. There's way too much psychology involved in what I was afraid of to go into here, but this agreement made perfect sense back then. And it worked. As I got more practice and increased the amount of time I was in conscious contact with God, being a conduit for *Love*, I began to absorb this new reality into my mind. My brain was most satisfied when I became able to describe what I was experiencing.

* * *

Even if we aren't consciously aware of it, our minds sense that everything must be balanced. If we are going to live our lives in a new and different way, there has to be something we lose for everything we gain. If we aren't actively thinking about this belief, we may not be able to explain our resistance to adopting a new way of being that we are convinced is beneficial for us.

I've said that the illusion of the world is addictive. Breaking a cycle of addiction can come at a steep price. It may cost us money, but it often costs us the friends we used to have. If alcohol was our addiction, we are most likely going to have to give up our old drinking buddies. If there were places we liked to go or activities that we enjoyed that had some association with drinking, we're going to have to give those things up as well. This is too great a price for some, and the addiction continues.

To drastically alter the way you think and decide to live a spiritual life in unity with *Love* is not a casual decision. There is work to do and difficulties to overcome. It may be difficult to start this journey if we're in a toxic situation. We may have to make some difficult choices. If we've enjoyed the drama we've experienced, despite knowing that it interferes with our desire to be filled with unconditional *Love*, it may seem a great price to give that up. Consciously and subconsciously, our minds weigh the options. If we are unsure what we may need to surrender to gain what we are after, a conflict can arise, and our minds sound an alarm.

It's a good idea to try to define what it is we want and figure out what it will take to get it. To keep our minds from sabotaging ourselves, we can make a deal with ourselves. We can give ourselves permission to walk away at any time, without judgment or remorse—but we can always pick up and try again later. This way, we give ourselves room to grow and a little bit of patience to do it.

You Can Refuse Any Thoughts You Don't Want

Many spiritual people have said this, and I'm going to say it, too: you can refuse to give power to any of your thoughts. If a destructive thought comes into your mind, acknowledge it, then refuse it. Say it out loud if you have to: "I refuse to give this thought any energy." And then be done with it. If it comes back, tell it you refuse it and to go away.

For example, I may have done something embarrassing. Perhaps I've done something that pushed away an opportunity I'd been looking for. Maybe I remember something I did long ago that hurt someone else. Many different thoughts can come from the judge in my mind to accuse and convict me. I might hear a thought that tells me I'm stupid or unworthy, or that I should feel guilty. I have three options: I can accept the accusations and assumptions in those thoughts; I can try to ignore them; or I can acknowledge them, then refuse them.

I may want to try something new, but fear and doubt come into my mind. I can listen to those thoughts and not try; I can try, but be constantly worried and not enjoy the journey; or I can tame those thoughts and refuse them.

I like to use the word *refuse* because it's active. It means that I am acknowledging the thing and then turning it away. I'm not trying to ignore it, because that takes more energy. Thoughts that go unaddressed can be very persistent and distracting. Instead, I recognize how my mind wants to work: I acknowledge the thought that comes to the forefront of my mind. If it's something that evokes a painful emotion, I can either dive deeper into it or simply refuse it.

As I practice this, I get better and better at recognizing thoughts that need to be shooed away. I've been caught saying "Nope," or "No thanks, you can go now" out loud! I've had to explain that I had a negative thought, and I was refusing it. When I first started doing this, I was amazed at how easy and effective it is.

Some thoughts come disguised as emotions. I treat them the same way. Instead of a thought of self-doubt or guilt, I get a feeling in my chest or stomach. I might get a flash of anger without a conscious thought. I can refuse those emotions as quickly and certainly as I would a thought I didn't welcome.

This is fundamental to taming the mind. It becomes easier with practice, but the only thing needed is willingness and the awareness that you are worthy of unconditional love. That's the basis on which the thoughts are rejected. I love myself unconditionally, which means I forgive myself unconditionally. What good does a thought or feeling of guilt do me? I know that my joy comes from the free flow of *Love* through me. What do I want with thoughts or feelings of anger or other negative energies that will only restrict or even block that flow?

You can start doing this right now. The next time you have a thought that tells you that you aren't good enough, acknowledge the thought with another thought: *I recognize this thought, but I refuse to accept it.* Then move on. At first, the subconscious mind doesn't know what to do with that, so it sends the thought back to the ego. Acknowledge it and refuse it again. I think (or sometimes say out loud), "Nope, don't need that," and go back to whatever it was I was doing.

This doesn't mean that every thought that causes a negative emotion should be refused. I may need to listen to the thought that says I shouldn't walk down a particular street alone at night. I might need to pay some attention to a guilty feeling if it means I need to make amends. But I don't need to dwell on a thought or accept the ones that tell me I'm something other than what I am.

There are always limitations to my physical and mental abilities. There are things I do well, things I cannot do, and things that fall somewhere in between. I may have limitations on my resources. None of those limitations, however, define who I am. I am not my abilities, either. My identity isn't tied to what I'm good or successful at. There are times when my mind throws a thought at me that seems like praise, but I refuse those, too. I am happy with who I am, and I don't need anyone—even my brain—to tell me I am one way or the other.

Just try it and see. When a thought comes into your mind that seems like it's trying to define you, acknowledge it, then refuse it. It doesn't matter if it's a "good" thought or a "bad" one. You are who you are. *Love* yourself the way you are right now. You are allowed to change, and you probably will. Who you are is something you feel and know, not what you think. The more we try to think about what we should be, the harder it becomes to be that way.

* * *

With our thoughts tamed, we have so much more energy to do what we enjoy and to enjoy what we do. We will recognize the opportunities around us and use them to make our lives and this world better. Without thoughts bringing us fear, we move through the world fearlessly. We see what we want, and we go for it. We see what we can do for others, and we do it without expecting anything in return. We don't invest our thoughts and emotions in an outcome, but stay within the moment, spending our energies on thoughts and actions that reinforce and enhance our joy.

Dealing with Anger

Anger comes in many forms, but no matter which way we feel it, anger is only fear on the offensive. Generally, anger represents the fear of losing something we have or not getting something we want. Sometimes, anger can be a result of some kind of perceived threat, but that, too, is based on the fear of losing something, whether it is our sense of security, our health, our relationships, or our possessions.

We can get angry over a disagreement with someone or with an ideology. While the current social and political climate in the world in the early twenty-first century seems filled with conflict and hatred, this really isn't anything new. People are afraid, and many people are afraid all the time. To defend against that *Fear*, we often rely on anger to feel some sense of control. *Fear* feels passive, and anger feels active.

But anger gives us a false sense of power and security. Like basic fear (worry, nervousness, terror), anger also pulls our attention away from the moment and causes our brains to operate differently. This is called the fight-or-flight response. This response can be triggered by threats real or imagined and can greatly impact the way we make decisions. Psychologists believe that this response is evolutionary, a built-in response to threats against our survival. When humans were hunter-gatherers, real threats existed from predators and competing tribes. But this response helps us quickly evaluate a mortal threat and act accordingly. In our modern social environment, however, this response may be triggered by threats not so much to our physical being, but to our overall survival, or even just our lifestyle.

In our social contexts, though, the fight-or-flight response pushes our decision-making ability into the immediate or short-term time frame, and those decisions may not be compatible with our long-term goals. For instance, if we are arguing with our partner, and the fear and anger within our mind builds up, that survival response can kick in. It is the argument itself that is creating the threat, and our response may be more aimed at stopping that argument than actually "winning" it. In those moments, we may say or do things that don't just stop the argument, but damage or even destroy the relationship.

* * *

Sometimes our anger stems from not feeling validated or acknowledged. I may feel like I have some very important information to share and that it is important for the person or people I'm sharing with to listen and agree. On the other hand, someone may try to share their ideas with me, and I firmly disagree with them. Our debate might become emotional and turn into an argument. There's an old saying: "Would you rather be happy, or rather be right?" The idea here is that whatever we're arguing about or trying to convince someone of probably isn't that important or worth getting angry about or hurting someone's feelings over.

A long time ago, I went to see a film called *Tombstone*.

It's a story about Wyatt Earp. In one scene, Wyatt (played by Kurt Russel) is being challenged by Johnny Ringo (Michael Biehn). Wyatt says to Johnny, "I won't fight you, Ringo; there's no money in it." That sentiment has stuck with me to this day. It's also been very helpful for keeping myself out of trouble.

The idea that "there's no money in it" may feel cold and detached, but it is simply to say that whatever it is I'm considering isn't beneficial. If I find myself in a conversation or situation where I can feel anger rising, I just ask myself, "Is there any money in it?" Again, "money" here doesn't mean cash; it just means benefit. If you and I are getting into a heated debate, it's useful for me to assess whether my position is beneficial. What difference does it make if we agree or disagree? Does it really matter if we don't believe the same things? I've found that in most cases, it's better to be happy than right—that there really isn't any gain in winning an argument.

That's not to say that there aren't times when arguing a point or position isn't necessary. There will be times when we have to stand up for what we believe in or defend ourselves. In those instances, it's also important to avoid taking things personally and allowing ourselves to lose objectivity through anger.

* * *

In dealing with anger, it's helpful to understand that anger is a form of *Fear*. So then, when we begin to feel angry, it's important to ask ourselves what it is we are afraid of. If we're angry because we've been embarrassed, humiliated, or disrespected, we are probably afraid of losing our social status or revealing the vulnerability of our ego. If someone insults me, I might become angry because I'm afraid the insult may be true. But no matter what I think I'm angry about, I'm really just reacting to some kind of fear. Now that I know my anger is a reaction to *Fear*, I can address the *Fear* itself.

There are times when it's best to take a step back and collect myself. If I'm in an argument with someone or getting angry at someone who isn't meeting my expectations, I may need to retreat. At the very least, I may need to stop talking. I may even need to tolerate verbal abuse—which is really hard, I know. But if I can get away and calm down, I can slow my thoughts down and quiet my mind. Then I can have a clearer view of what I'm afraid of and what I felt threatened by.

* * *

There are times when anger comes on so fast that there isn't any time to avoid it. Driving in rush-hour traffic is a great place to get annoyed and angry in an instant. Poor or even rude service in a restaurant is another. A disobedient or petulant child. Experiencing an injustice. How do we deal with these things that come on suddenly? Do we perform some analysis after the fact, when we have time to calm down? Well, the best thing we can do for ourselves is to not get angry in the first place, regardless of the circumstance.

Anger is a reaction to *Fear* and is a product of our evolution as a species. We can see similar behavior in other mammals, especially the social ones, like dogs, apes, and monkeys. What separates humans from animals, though, is ego. The fear of any threat to our sense of self, self-importance, or the façade we've created to protect ourselves adds another target and another layer of complexity. Regardless of the source (or the complexity), anger is a secondary emotion, usually a response to *Fear*, but it may also be a response to and defense against other emotions, such as sadness.

It's fairly easy to train ourselves to react with a question rather than an emotion. It just takes practice. Make the decision to question your anger every time you feel it. At first, it may take a while before you begin to question your own responses and emotions. The more you do, though, the quicker you will question your own reactions. Eventually, it becomes automatic. Long before I found my spirituality, driving in heavy traffic was often a source of aggravation and anger for me. I became habituated to getting angry when I perceived someone doing something rude, stupid, aggressive, or dangerous on the road. To this day, I can be caught off guard and get angry at another driver before I've questioned the emotion. But as soon as I do, I quickly realize that my anger is a response to the *Fear* that I felt in the moment.

Another way to put this is that we can create a gatekeeper or a filter in our minds. That gatekeeper can stop the anger before it gains strength, and interrogate it. "What was I afraid of that caused me to respond with anger?" It isn't critically important that we answer that question accurately; the important part is that we pause long enough to recapture the energy we're about to waste. We're reclaiming our ability to make rational and informed decisions rather than react without thinking of the consequences. It does help if we can accurately identify the fear that evoked the anger, but that is secondary.

* * *

Another tool we can use to help ourselves deal with anger—especially its aftermath—is forgiveness and self-love. When I've reacted out of anger, or made important decisions while angry, I've often come to regret it. I've said hurtful things to people. I've destroyed sentimental possessions. I've damaged or dissolved relationships. I've quit or lost good jobs. I've done a lot of damage to myself and the people I care for because I let my fear and anger fuel my actions and decisions. This creates new opportunities for regret and anger at oneself. I've had to make amends many times for things I've said or done because I acted out of anger.

When we dig ourselves into a hole of regret and remorse, it can be pretty hard to get out of it. It can be difficult to feel like we're even worthy of forgiveness. We may punish ourselves repeatedly. We may avoid meaningful relationships because we've lost trust in ourselves. This is where we desperately need self-forgiveness.

When we make amends for our bad behavior, it isn't to gain forgiveness, but to give the other person the *opportunity* to forgive. There is no guarantee that they will, but in some cases, we have an obligation to open the door. There are times, though, when the damage we've done is so great that the best amends we can make is to stay away. There is no patented formula to help us decide what's appropriate for every instance where we have hurt someone. Regardless, we owe ourselves forgiveness, too. Forgiveness opens the door and allows *Love* to flow through us. Guilt (a form of *Fear*) blocks that flow, keeps us from experiencing the richness of life, and prevents us from expressing that gift to others. But *Love* brings with it a greater understanding of the world around us and the people in it.

Toxic People, Psychic Vampires, and Trolls

In this digital age, we have a greater opportunity to come into contact with a more diverse population. We can communicate with people we'd otherwise never get to experience or know. But with the advent of social media, we have discovered a new monster: the "troll." They are the internet version of psychic vampires (also called energy vampires). They use their own toxicity to bore holes into your mind from which they can drain your emotional energy. Anyone can at any time be a troll, an energy vampire, or toxic—and all at the same time.

The capacity to be toxic exists in all of us and always comes from a place of fear and pain. There is absolutely no way that a person can intentionally hurt someone for the purpose of feeding off of their negative emotions, and also be filled with *Love*. The longer someone practices such toxicity, the harder it will be for them to either find that place of *Love* within themselves, or return to it if they had found it at one time.

The more I put my name out in public, the greater the number of trolls who will come for my energy. It isn't personal; it's just something they need to feel better (or to feel something at all). They are after power, not just energy. They need to feel the control of manipulating another human into feeling as terrible inside as they are. Some are suffering from mental disorders that drive them to be cruel, sarcastic, and toxic. Some are jealous, and rather than lift themselves up, they tear others down.

I have heard and have given the advice to cut toxic people out of our lives. For those who are just beginning their journey to spiritual awareness and healing, I stand by this advice. While you are connecting with your spiritual self and winding your way to filling yourself with unconditional *Love*, it is most important to take care of yourself and remove yourself from the *Fear* energy of hatred. Until we can tame our thoughts, we need to avoid the temptation to return the poison we receive with more poison of our own.

I added online trolls to this list because in that semi-anonymous world, it is too easy to respond to toxicity with equal or greater force. But because our posts are public, it is easy to be embarrassed and concerned with our image if we let an insult or criticism go unchallenged. We may fear our credibility will be damaged if we don't respond.

Sometimes, when I encounter trolls online, my ego jumps up from its resting place and demands a response. That, however, is just that: ego. I have to remind myself that it's nothing personal. I can instead use it as an opportunity to communicate better. Maybe I could have said something better. Maybe I didn't think that what I said could touch a nerve. Maybe it's just fine and there's nothing more to it. Regardless, how someone reacts isn't anything I can control. If I am intent on sharing what I believe in and have to offer, I must accept the risk that some people are going to see that as a challenge or an opportunity to drain my energy. It's nothing personal, and I have to remember that. If I can't, I need to back away until I can.

When I get to the point where I don't take myself so seriously—when I know who I am and have sent my ego into the background—I can immunize myself against the toxins people try to inject me with. Most of the time, I simply do not react at all. I am confident in what I am doing and what I am saying, and I know what I am trying to accomplish is good. I can take feedback, I can examine criticism, and I can find something useful in every comment, regardless of the intent of the sender. When a comment touches a nerve, that's the most useful feedback I can get, because it tells me directly where I need to focus my energy and what I need to heal.

There are times, too, when I must respond with love, patience, and kindness, and acknowledge that person. It isn't always easy to tell if someone is truly an energy vampire or just letting me know that they are in pain and need some help. That is a very delicate balance, to be sure. No matter how well practiced I am in my spirituality, I am still human, with a lifetime of egocentricity under my belt. Some habits die hard, and I am not always able to tell if I'm being asked for help or being baited. When I am not sure, I find it best to be quiet. I accept, too, that I cannot help everyone that I would like to, and that my help may not be welcome, or even be the help a person needs. If they are sincere about finding their path to a happier existence, I trust that the universe offers them the same opportunities that it gave to me.

There are still people I encounter from time to time that I just have to push away or stay away from (or block online). There are some whose fear and anger are very practiced and powerful. They are masters of hurting people and feeding off whatever fearful energy gets returned. Responding to them is priming the pump, and they will pump until their host is drained; then they move on, but will likely return when your energy is somewhat restored. Not only am I not obligated to take abuse, it is also irresponsible to do so. There are times when the best thing I can do for someone is to disengage and refuse to allow them access to my energy. If the power of *Fear* is so great within them that they cannot receive the *Love* that I or anyone else would send to them, then there is nothing I can do to help them. *Love* must be given and accepted freely. It cannot be forced on anyone who would not have it.

I've often wondered why I ever chose to live as a toxic person or an energy vampire myself. Why would I crave that energy at all when all it brings is heartache, pain, isolation, and loneliness? I am grateful that I wasn't that way all the time, but there were times when I acted that way and fed off people's anger—usually justified by a desire for revenge of some kind. But I did do that, and I do know what it feels like. I understand it to a degree, though that understanding isn't universal. In my case, I just didn't have any connection to the love inside me that was buried under layers of pain, fear, and anger. I craved that energy, though I couldn't identify it and didn't know what it was, but I did know of another energy—the kind that comes from fear, anger, and pain.

Instinctively, I knew I could draw that energy from someone else and recharge my emotional batteries, if only just a bit. But besides the obvious problem of hurting other people (regardless of what they may have done or not done to me), that energy is a finite resource. It gets used up and has to be replenished, or the vampire gets swept away in their own despair. I believe that most of the time, the people who are trying to gain that energy from others are simply desperate. They are stuck in their misery and don't know how to get out. They want love, but haven't found it within themselves and may not believe that they are worthy, and so they reject love in favor of the only other energy they can get from others: fear. I suppose this is the basis of the saying, "Misery loves company."

There is no obligation in our spiritual awareness or spiritual health to keep toxic people in our lives. It's great if we can help someone find a better, happier way, but that is not our responsibility, and it doesn't actually matter. We are all made of the same stuff, the same energy. We are here for a time, and then we are not. Our energy, though, returns to the universe in another form. That is true regardless of how we choose to spend this time, whether we are happy or not.

The choice to live in the warm light of *Love* is just that: a choice. Whether that is better or worse is a matter of perspective, and it is far from me to judge or decide what is best or better for anyone else. My path is my path. My joy is my joy. I love sharing what I have because I love what I have, and I know that many other people will enjoy it and share it, too. But I am not so arrogant as to think that this is the only way or even the best way—or that someone whom I think is miserable, because I felt miserable when I behaved that way, is worse off than I am. It may sound strange or completely backward, but some people are very happy being miserable. Some people experience their joy in their *Fear* and wish to share and spread it as much as I want to share and spread the *Love* that I have inside me.

There is yet another component to this. I've mentioned a few times that in unconditional *Love,* without judgment and with a willingness to forgive, there is respect. In that, we respect others to tell their story however they see fit. That means that I don't judge the rightness or wrongness of their story. My belief and my spirituality say that I benefit when I love someone without conditions, judgments, or expectations, just the way that they are and not how I wish them to be. In fact, I ought not to wish anyone to be different from how they are. That is not my purpose and is way outside of my boundaries.

The best that I can do for anyone else is to be authentic and honest. If people find that attractive and want to know how they can have something of what I have, then I am honored to share what I know, however I can, whenever I can. According to my belief system, then, by the code I have chosen, my responsibility is to love you, no matter what, and not judge you for who you are trying to be. That may not always be easy with some of the people we encounter in life, but the reward for giving *Love* instead of returning poison is immeasurable.

Patience

Patience is a natural side effect of being present. Impatience is the result of being invested in an outcome. If I am doing what I need to do now, then the outcome is irrelevant. I am happy and satisfied in this moment, so there is no reason for me to build up expectations. Whatever will happen will happen, but experience tells me that I have a better chance of realizing my goals if I'm not burning off energy worrying or trying to row against the tide.

When I release my expectations and detach my emotions from the outcome of whatever I'm after, I'm focusing instead on the present moment in my journey. I know that my goal isn't yet realized at that moment, but I also know that I am moving toward my target. There is no room for impatience as long as I stay focused on *right now*.

I'm writing this book. It's taken me a long time to get to this point, and it can be tempting to build up scenarios and expectations for what I think the outcome should be. I may want to be finished and move on to the next phase. If I do that, I'm not going to give this my best, because my attention will be split between the words I'm typing and the words that will be printed. I'll probably miss something vital, something I want to tell you that I won't be able to if I spend time thinking about the other things that need to be done. I know what needs to be done; I don't need to keep reminding myself of it and try to rush into it. Seriously, people who were conceived at the same time as this book are in high school now! What are a few more weeks to make sure I give you my best?

Impatience is a form of worry, and worry is a form of *Fear*. It indicates that the flow of *Love* is restricted. Impatience is anticipation with the engine warmed up. It's ready to go. Ironically, impatience is a fear of not having what I don't have—the fear that I won't get what I want when I want it.

We can be impatient about all kinds of things, such as getting stuck in traffic or a long line at the checkout counter. We can get impatient when someone doesn't understand what we're saying or asking for. In every case, impatience happens when our minds are pushed into the future rather than being present in this moment.

* * *

Impatience can be a stumbling block along our spiritual journey, too. I have experienced this many times, and the result is always the same: I have to wait longer than I wanted.

The best cure for impatience is acceptance and self-love. Depending on where and how far you want to take your spiritual journey, there are certain natural effects of having awareness and conscious contact with the *Source*. Among them is the ease of staying in the moment. We are naturally unafraid and free from worry when we are not tied to the past or invested in an unrealized, nonexistent future. We have a keen awareness that there are no guarantees that what we want or anticipate will materialize—and that's okay.

The Only Time is Now

We can remember the past and imagine the future, but the only moment that truly exists is now. Now doesn't even exist in our thoughts, since the moment has already passed by the time we are able to realize and think of it. There is, however, a way to experience the present spiritually and allow the mind to be aware of it.

Whether we are aware or not, our physical form and our spirit are always in the present moment. It is only in the mind, in our thoughts, where time is skewed on either side of now. Our minds have us constantly reliving our past and rehearsing our future. Ironically, because our memories are so unreliable, our vision of the past may be just as inaccurate as our predictions and wishes.

We are bound to the now, but a lifetime of conditioning forces our thoughts into an alternate timeline. While our true self can be nowhere else but the present, our minds would have us all over the place, always trying to manipulate space and time, if only in our imaginations.

The key is to become aware of this moment. Our true, spiritual self is inseparably connected to the only moment that truly exists. The mind, however, is in conflict with this because it constantly builds a universe around the moment that has just passed, filled with so many possibilities and assumptions. I can know what city I'm in and the address I'm at. I can know what day and time it is. Yet, my mind is full of the things that I must do today, the people I need to talk to, the meals I need to eat, the transportation I need to take to get where I need to go. I'm thinking about conversations I've had and will have. I'm thinking about the mistakes I've made and how I should fix them. I'm thinking about how to impress someone. I'm thinking about someone who let me down.

Past and future collide and ricochet around my skull. I have too many thoughts to even enjoy the moment of now; I'm consciously disconnected from it. I think I can see the past and the near future, but I'm blinded to the only moment that exists or that will ever exist: now.

* * *

So, how do we get from there to here? Like any other journey, it begins with willingness, then practice. The first step is to recognize the thoughts that distract us from this moment. Thoughts of the future are tough, because we do have responsibilities, goals, and dreams. We must make plans and take steps and seize opportunities to achieve what we set out to do. But even though it sounds counterintuitive, focusing our existence in the now will help us accomplish what we want or need. In fact, once you decide you want something, you don't have to think about it again. You just need to take action, with one caveat: do not become emotionally invested in the outcome.

We can spend so much unnecessary and useless time trying to figure out how to manipulate the future. Who do I need to talk to? What do I need to say? What city should I live in? Which job should I try to get? What education do

I need? Summed up in a single question: what do I need to do to get from here to there? The answer to that question comes in a flurry of so many thoughts that it's a wonder we can get anything done at all. But there is a follow-up question to all those other questions: what are you willing to give up to get what you want? Time, money, friends, family, reputation—all these things can be up for grabs. There must be a balance to all accounts, and the mind is well aware of this. Along with all the other thoughts flying around, there is a weighing on the scales going on either consciously or subconsciously.

It is in that balancing that we get into the most trouble. How can I have my cake and eat it, too? How can I maximize my profit? This is where the fear of loss or failure creeps in. That is how we get trapped in a future that doesn't exist by constantly trying to manipulate people and situations to conform with that vision. Maybe it will work out, maybe it won't, but the possibility of failure despite all our efforts generates toxic worry and fear—sometimes to the point that we just give up or don't try at all.

The most significant damage is done when we wrap our identity up in the things we want to accomplish tomorrow. "I will be better when I have such and such." "Life will be so much easier/better." When we invest our identity in the outcome of a goal or dream, we run the risk of losing ourselves to an unfavorable outcome. If we link our sense of self to some vision of the future, what happens to our identity when we reach the end of that path? Whether the outcome is infinitely better than what we could have imagined, or a total catastrophe, where does that leave the I?

There is a way, though, to make plans and accomplish goals without the attachment and loss of the self. If you know what it is you want, or where it is you want to be, then you probably have a pretty good idea of what that would look like. If you can imagine that, you can imagine how you would feel if you were already in that situation. Instead of chasing that feeling, simply imagine yourself in that situation right now. Keep that in focus in the present—not as something to be accomplished, but as something already attained.

That is the Law of Attraction (also called manifesting) in a nutshell. I want to say here and now that there is no magic behind the Law of Attraction or manifesting. There is a simple, psychological basis to its methods that helps you see opportunities beyond obstacles. It's a great way to remove "can't" and "never" from our active thoughts. I use similar techniques in my teaching, and they can be useful, but I want to be abundantly clear: this isn't attracting anything; it's merely blowing away the fog that prevents us from seeing opportunities as they exist at the moment. The fog is the cacophony of a thousand simultaneous conflicting thoughts, and it is those thoughts that prevent us from focusing on the now.

By detaching our emotions from the outcome, we allow ourselves to join with the flow of time rather than fight against it. If success is guaranteed, it will come when it comes. If there is a chance of missing the mark, that will come when it comes, too. If we know what the goal is and generally what the prerequisites are, there is no need to fill our heads with stressful thoughts. But if we are emotionally attached to the outcome, those thoughts will be impossible to avoid.

Instead, we can try something else. Let's imagine that I want to manage a bookstore, or maybe even own one. Right now, I don't know very much about management or how to run a retail business, but I have a passion for books, and I am interested in people who are passionate about books, too. Obviously, there are steps I must take to prepare the way. How should I go about this? Should I dive in headfirst, or take a slower, more methodical approach?

To begin, I refuse to become emotionally invested in the outcome. What matters is my conscious contact with the *Source* and the joy that brings. The bookstore becomes ornamental. It is not a thing I need, but a thing I want to experience. I don't know if the business will succeed or fail, but I don't need to worry about it. If I begin to worry about the outcome, I'm very likely to miss the opportunities that will serve my goal the best.

I know what I want to do. My energy, then, can be spent learning about practical things that go into the operation of a bookstore. I don't need to keep telling myself I want to run a bookstore, because that's already been established. It would be very helpful, too, if I refused thoughts that provoke fear and worry.

Give Yourself the Freedom and Permission to Just Be

Practicing anything has its share of successes and failures. Some days are better than others. The effect of our best efforts may change from day to day, depending on our physical, emotional, mental, and spiritual health. Sometimes we can slip and wobble, and other times we can hit the floor—hard.

Give yourself permission to fail, and also to succeed. Success may be a lot harder to define and envision than failure. Whatever it is that we might call "success" may come as the greater surprise, and we might not know what to do with it. That is why giving yourself permission to succeed is just as important as permission to fail. This permission helps us stay present in the moment. It allows us to accept life on life's terms, and it returns the energy we expend on anxiety and self-doubt. We are really giving ourselves permission to enjoy the experience of learning and growing without anchoring ourselves to an outcome. When we give ourselves permission to experience things, we free ourselves from judgment, and all this allows the attempt to be just as wonderful as what we are trying to accomplish.

Whenever you feel like you've had a setback, acknowledge the emotion, then refuse it. Remember instead that you have permission to enjoy the experience, no matter what. It's been said that there are no failures, only learning opportunities. If you understand that there is no other moment than the one you are in now, you will see that you cannot fail to be who you are. Whatever is going on that blocks the flow of *Love* is just something else to be experienced. You *are*. That's it. What you do with your time here is for you to decide and to enjoy, or not enjoy. You are allowed to do with it whatever you want. There is no right or wrong way. Instead, there is joy and pain. You get to decide which you want most, and then you get to figure out the rest.

When a child is first learning to walk, it isn't helpful to punish the child for stumbling and falling down. We encourage the child, or better, we simply help them learn. We naturally give the child permission to stumble and fall. We ought to treat ourselves the same way. We are learning, practicing, and doing, sometimes well, sometimes not. There is no reason to bring down judgment.

Finally, if we give ourselves permission to experience the journey, win or lose, succeed or fail, then no matter what happens, forgiveness is automatic. The judge has no power to interfere with our joy, and we will be happy no matter what.

Chapter Fifteen: *Enlightenment*

"The word enlightenment conjures up the idea of some superhuman accomplishment, and the ego likes to keep it that way, but it is simply your natural state of felt oneness with Being."

— *Eckhart Tolle*

The End of Suffering

The word *enlightenment* can mean different things to different people. The definition of the word is "a state of having great knowledge." Enlightenment comes to us through our practice, prayer, and meditation, but it is never complete. The old mystic Rajneesh said:

> "Enlightenment is finding that there is nothing to find. Enlightenment is to come to know that there is nowhere to go. Enlightenment is the understanding that this is all, that this is perfect, that this is it. Enlightenment is not an achievement, it is an understanding that there is nothing to achieve, nowhere to go. You are already there—you have never been away. You cannot be away from there. God has never been missed. Maybe you have forgotten,

that's all. Maybe you have fallen asleep,
that's all."

Enlightenment isn't a destination; it is an understanding. It begins where you do. As soon as you start to realize who and what you really are, you have enlightenment, and you will likely become more enlightened. You will know more about the universe and our place in it than you did before.

Transcendence

The idea of transcendence is ancient. For thousands of years, spiritualists, thinkers, and philosophers have debated what transcendence means and if or how it can be achieved. But what is transcendence? In simple terms, transcendence is an experience beyond the physical and psychological. It is a state of being that transcends what we understand as "normal" or usual. There are many schools of thought and practice that claim to lead to transcendence, or deny it altogether.

There are ancient texts, such as the *Lotus Sutra*, that try to define enlightenment and poetically describe the struggle to achieve it. Depending on what you read or whom you listen to, enlightenment and transcendence are rare and difficult to achieve. I could not disagree more. It isn't the achievement of transcendence that is difficult; the hard part is the decision to let go of everything you've thought you are.

Anyone with the intellectual and emotional capacity to take inventory of themselves and their lives is capable of true and complete enlightenment. The key requirements are self-awareness and absolute honesty. I have no idea how much cognitive ability, emotional maturity, mental illness, or impairment factor into the attainment of enlightenment and transcendence, or even if such things do. I am certain, however, that most humans can indeed achieve a transcendent state of being.

I've stated many times that there must always be balance in the universe. For something gained, there is something lost. This is just the nature of the universe itself: there is a finite amount of energy that cannot be created nor destroyed, only converted from one form to another. Because of that, even on an ethereal level, there must always be balance. This is unavoidable.

The totality of the universe and the energy that makes it exist is *Love*. This energy isn't just a force; it is *the* force, and it is the only thing that truly exists in purity. Transcendence, then, brings us into harmony with that force. It brings us into unity with *Love*.

There is no single formula for how to attain transcendence. There are practices and philosophies that, over the course of human history, have proved helpful to that aim. But each path is unique; none, no matter how similar, are the same. Nothing in this book should be considered a guide to transcendence. If that is something you seek, you will find your way. My goal here, though, is to explain as best I can what I believe transcendence to be and what it costs.

There is nothing good or bad about being transcendent. It is unqualifiable. I would say that, from a non-transcendent perspective, the most relatable feeling would be that of absolute and unending ecstasy, bliss beyond bliss. That sounds pretty awesome because, well, it is. Why, then, wouldn't everyone want to live like that? Is it so hard to achieve because it's so amazing?

In all the teachings I've studied, I have identified two

main types of transcendence. One is like swimming in a pool; it's something you do from time to time. The other is like becoming the water in the pool.

Let's look at the first and most common type of transcendence: the dip in the pool. Through practice, patience, and meditation, we can relieve ourselves of the ego self and experience the immense joy of being in tune with the universe and with the energy of *Love*. We give ourselves over to pure and perfect *Love*. We release our ego and realize our true nature, our true selves as *being* the universe itself. In that state, there is a moment of connectedness and awareness that transcends our normal state of being. For however long we can sustain it, we are floating in the pure water that is the essence of life. We vibrate with the hum of the universe, and we experience the pure bliss of being one with everything that is. It is in this space where we know the unknowable. Here we see the beginning and end of everything that exists. If we wish, we can push our consciousness into eternity and be one with it, too.

From there, we can even go from being the swimmer to being the water. This is where the big question comes: if it's so great, why not just go? Well, some have, and some will. It's just that in that space, in that awareness, the cost becomes perfectly clear: we have to leave everything behind and never come back. In other words, it's a one-way trip.

If you seek enlightenment, just trust that you will achieve it, and you will achieve it. If you seek transcendence, in the same way, trust that you will attain it, and you will attain that, too. It takes a lot of work and a lot of reprogramming.

Most of all, it takes a strong will and the willingness to let go of things once valued.

I don't recall ever actively seeking to be in a transcendent state. It's something that happened as a result of deep and persistent meditation. I have no recipe for how to achieve such a state directly. The only common thread between the few times that I have felt transcendent is the complete dissociation of self and an immense connection to the energy of *Love* that I felt. There was no emotion, no joy, no attachment, no elation—nothing. It was the purest awareness of existence I have experienced.

It can (and should) be a lot of fun to be human. Whether I've had past lives or will have others, this is the only one I'm aware of right now. This is the life I'm living in this moment, and this, therefore, is the one that matters. Enlightenment has given me the awareness that pain is inevitable, but suffering is optional. In fact, according to the Buddha, enlightenment means the end of suffering. With this awareness, I can go a step further and experience something beyond myself.

The awareness of enlightenment informs me of my attachments. Because my love for myself and others is unconditional, there is no judgment about my attachments. I care about what I care about. I enjoy what I enjoy. And though I try to release any expectations of permanence, I want to hang onto the things I care about and enjoy. The price I pay for that is the risk of experiencing grief and disappointment. But I'm willing to pay that price and am content with that decision.

Could I be "happier" in transcendence? That depends on what "happier" means, but sure, I could. Absolute ecstasy sounds marvelous, but I don't think it's better or worse than any other way of being. I'm not sure if I can truly express what I believe the cost of pure transcendence is, because I'm not sure it's the same for everyone or everything. For me, the ultimate cost is letting go of all my relationships. Granted, in such a state of being, I wouldn't really care about that, because such things become meaningless. Affection is about the ego and the self. Everything—every particle of energy—is equal in the context of transcendent unity with the universe. Importance is meaningless, because it doesn't exist without the concept of self.

Transcendence, then, is meaningless. I don't say that to qualify it; it's not good, and it's not bad. It just is. Being transcendent isn't better than anything else. It isn't worse than anything else. It just is. In this way, it's only a choice.

I want to say here that "meaningless" doesn't mean "hopeless." Meaning is a concept created from perception. Meaning and meaninglessness are subjective and relative. It's paradoxical but accurate to say that we can have a meaningful, meaningless existence, because it is our perspective and our will that create meaning in our lives. You and only you can give your life meaning. Only you can define the value in your life and everything in it. That value is based on the balance you've chosen to create within your life, even if you aren't conscious and aware of it.

Does that mean that transcendence isn't worth the effort? Not at all. There is a lot to be gained from the experience, even if it doesn't make anything about us better.

I suppose the best thing I can say about my transcendent experiences is that they've helped me not take myself too seriously. I forgive myself for harmful thoughts and mistakes more readily. I forgive others more quickly. I can appreciate this fleeting life a bit more.

* * *

There are times and events in our lives that can awaken us to the truth of the universe and life itself. There are moments that can bring us into transcendence without us having to try. We can also work to attain a transcendent state. And while transcendent experiences can positively impact and enrich our lives, they aren't necessary in order for us to achieve the one thing most of us want: happiness and serenity.

The one thing I'd love to give to every human being that ever was or ever will be is the awareness of unconditional *Love*. Within that awareness is the understanding that we hold within ourselves the keys to happiness and serenity, and the knowledge that our very presence on this planet can bring peace and joy to others.

Hidden Wisdom

I want to mention something that you may or may not experience, but if you do, it can be helpful to have an idea of what you are experiencing. In the fullness of *Love* (conscious contact with God), there is a certain wisdom that I call the *River of Knowledge*. The celebrated psychotherapist Carl Jung called it the "collective unconscious." It flows within our unconscious mind and is part of every living thing. When our minds are quiet and in harmony with *Love*, we have conscious access to that knowledge.

Some of this knowledge we can keep and share with others. Some of it we can't. Some of this knowledge is often not transferable or translatable. I've tried to relate things I found in the *River of Knowledge* in real time, but the people listening to me just heard jumbles of words with little meaning. I know what I wanted to relay to them; I just didn't have the words to say it. I suspect, however, that their own collective unconscious—their *River of Knowledge*—was able to interpret what I said.

Most of what I've found in that knowledge is helpful in understanding why we're here in the first place. I am able to keep that knowledge when I'm not in the flow. Some things, however, evaporate if I move away from my conscious contact with the *Source*. I remember knowing things, and I remember what it felt like to know those things, I just can't remember what those things were. I call that the "unknowable knowledge." It's like a reference book at a library that you can read while you're there, but can't check out. You can make some copies and jot down some notes, but those are just fragments. To get back to that knowledge, you have to go back to the library. Spiritual awareness is like that. While our awareness is energized and *Love* is flowing freely through and from us, we have easy access to that knowledge. But if we give in to *Fear*—either by accident or by choice—then we also lose access to most of that wisdom.

This helps explain why there are so many different religions, myths, and spiritual teachings from all over the world that say much the same thing: God is *Love*. The only thing that truly exists is *Love. Love* is pure energy. We are in God, and God is in us. We are one. What we perceive is an illusion. All of these ideas flow from the *River of Knowledge*.

* * *

Sometimes when you meditate and you've quieted your thoughts and turned your focus to *Love*, you will have a moment where you suddenly understand something that you heard or read. During a time of profound unity with *Love*, I read the Christian Bible again, but what I got out of it was nothing like I expected. I saw the meaning of things written, though poorly translated in places, that I'd never noticed before. I noticed that much of the wisdom survived clerical errors and biases in translation. I was able to see past the doctrine I'd studied years earlier. The same was true for other texts I enjoyed, from ancient Eastern writings to the works of modern spiritual teachers.

There is no shortcut to the *River of Knowledge*. It is something that exists within a quieted mind and in the fullness of connection with *Love*. Therefore, connecting to hidden wisdom isn't necessary for the journey. It is helpful for the mind, because the human mind has a very hard time accepting the abstract nature of transcendence. In a way, the *River of Knowledge* keeps the mind occupied and interested. While having a fulfilling conscious contact with and awareness of *Love* is the most blissful, peaceful, and fearless feeling I've ever known, to a mind that is used to drama, it can seem rather boring. Access to the wisdom of the ages, however, is not boring—especially since there is seemingly infinite knowledge to consider.

I want to take a moment to say that this is nothing mystical or magical. Jung wrote of the collective unconscious, "My thesis, then, is as follows: In addition to our immediate consciousness, which is of a thoroughly personal nature and which we believe to be the only empirical psyche (even if we tack on the personal unconscious as an appendix), there exists a second psychic system of a collective, universal, and impersonal nature which is identical in all individuals. This collective unconscious does not develop individually but is inherited. It consists of pre-existent forms, the archetypes, which can only become conscious secondarily and which give definite form to certain psychic contents."

Most of us, at one time or another, have experienced a connection to our internal collective unconscious. This is where our instincts come from. When we have a feeling of danger when there is nothing we can detect with our senses, this is unconscious knowledge that evolved for our survival. Those that had such instincts survived. Those that didn't were eaten by animals or killed by their enemies. Another example is that sometimes we may visit a place for the first time, but we feel a familiarity with it and innately know how to get around and find places we shouldn't otherwise be able to.

I truly do not think there is anything magical about the collective unconscious. This is something that's baked into every human being—and likely every living thing. Personally, this isn't something that I actively pursue. Accessing it is merely a byproduct of quieting my mind in an effort to connect to something I enjoy more: pure, unconditional, spiritual love.

I cannot stress enough that tapping into this *River of Knowledge*—or hidden wisdom—is, like transcendence itself, of little importance in the journey to and practice of spiritual enlightenment. It doesn't add to or detract from the experience in any way. It's just something that might happen—or it might not. It makes no difference, and if you don't experience it, you aren't missing out on anything. I came very close to not including this in the book, but I thought it might be important to mention in case someone experiences it and is confused by it.

Chapter Sixteen: *We Are Gods*

*"When we know what God is, we
shall be gods ourselves."*

— *George Bernard Shaw*

Your God and You're God

Things were much easier when I preached the Gospel of Jesus Christ. I had the license to tell you who and what your God is, what He is about, and what He expects of you. Oh, such simpler times! As a minister, I believed my solemn duty was to inform, instruct, and guide people on their spiritual journeys. As a preacher, people looked to me for guidance and some glimmer of insight into what God wants from us.

The truth is, I have no business in telling you how to imagine the divine. Looking back, I think I always knew I had no business fashioning a god for other people. I was a lousy evangelist. My strongest skill was in bringing the people who'd fallen away back to church. I also had a gift for explaining scripture in a way that made sense.

I believe it is vital to have a real and personal relationship with a power greater than ourselves. For me, that is the energetic force of creation that I call *Love*. I also call that force God. I revere and respect this force, and I commune with it. I feel that I understand it and that it understands me; at the very least, it loves me just the way

I am, no matter what. I believe that we were all created to be one with this force. We came from that energy, and we will return to it. We can all tap into this energy and enjoy heaven on earth.

Just because I see God my way doesn't mean anyone else has to see God the same. My experience within the church showed me that, even among a congregation of believers, there were stark differences in how people perceived their god and creator. Some might envision a Zeus-like figure armed with thunder and lightning, full of wrath. Others might see a gentle spirit in sandals, sharing love and hope. Some might imagine a combination of the two or something different.

What I know is that it's up to you how you define your god. It's up to you to decide if you even want a god in your life. I find it makes my flavor of spirituality a bit easier to believe in, believing in a pure force of *Love*. Still, that's just how I've modeled it.

Even if we had irrefutable evidence of the divine, and it was spelled out and defined in explicit detail, no one would have the same understanding as anyone else. Humans aren't wired that way. Our perceptions are filtered through the lens of our thoughts and experiences and can change from day to day, moment to moment. We see things differently when we're sick than we do when we are well. We perceive details differently when we are happy than we do when we're sad. Even if we followed all the liturgy and ritual to the finest detail, our beliefs would be at least slightly different, and that difference redefines the god of our understanding.

I refuse to accept that the God of creation is moody, inconsistent, selective, jealous, or angry, or would create anything out of *Love* only to allow it to be tormented. I deny any god that is supposed to be all-loving on the one hand, and on the other is compelled to resort to threats and extortion to keep worshipers in line. However, I do not judge or resent anyone who believes in such a deity. It's their business, and it's their relationship. It doesn't matter what I think or believe; their beliefs are their own. Yours are your own to do with as you please.

This can be a touchy subject, to be sure. Some people can get defensive about their dogma—even violently so. Some people might feel that any description of a god other than their own ideal is offensive. From a psychological perspective, it's understandable. If Jane has her image of God, and Joe comes along and describes something wildly different, Jane may feel like Joe is accusing her of being a fool or lying. Joe doesn't have to say anything like that, but there is a chance that the accusation is implied and perceived. There are those, too, who are genuinely concerned for your immortal soul; it would help if you believed as they do to secure your place in heaven. Otherwise, you could burn in the fires of hell. They're truly afraid on behalf of those they consider lost.

If I am asked (and by reading this book, I'll consider that you are interested), I will share what I believe. It is not my intent to break anyone's faith or take their god away from them. Unconditional love is just that, and if that's what I want to espouse, I am obliged to accept people—and their beliefs—just as they are. I absolutely will not argue or apologize for my beliefs. That serves no good purpose.

I want to make abundantly clear that you are allowed to see your god your way. You are free and welcome to adopt any form that god might take and practice any religion you are comfortable with. You are in control of your mind and your thoughts, and you are responsible for your spiritual wellbeing. That is between you and your god—and it's nobody else's business.

* * *

When I use the word *God*, I am also referring to *Love*. When I use the word *Love*, I also refer to the *Source*. If I were to compare these words to the Christian Trinity, I would say that the Father is God, Jesus is the *Source*, and *Love* is the Holy Spirit. They all refer to certain qualities of the same thing. *God*, *Source*, and *Love* can be used interchangeably, but each word carries its own connotations because of the nuances of language. Each word contains a different image or implies a different function, but the whole functions as one.

Many religions and spiritual teachings accept that we as individuals are somehow broken off from the *Source* or otherwise separated from God, and that there is a path to be reunited. I do not think we are separated from God, but we are often unaware of our connection to Him, or our godhood. Even the Bible supports this idea. Psalm 82:6 reads, " 'You are gods, all of you are sons of the Most High.' " When Jesus was being accused of blasphemy for saying he was the Son of God, he replied to his accusers, "[34] Isn't it written in your law, 'I said, you are gods?' [35] If he called them gods, to whom the word of God came (and the Scripture can't be broken), [36] do you say of him whom the father sanctified and sent into the world, 'You blaspheme,' because I said, 'I am the Son of God?'" (John 10:34-36, *World English Bible*).

George Bernard Shaw was onto something when he said, "When we know what God is, we shall be gods ourselves." Accepting your divinity, though, maybe a bit hard to swallow, at least at first. Still, it is essential that you do. In his book, *The Mastery of Love: A Practical Guide to Personal Freedom,* Don Miguel Ruiz shares his version of an old tale:

> There is an old story from India about the God, Brahma, who was all alone. Nothing existed but Brahma, and he was completely bored. Brahma decided to play a game, but there was no one to play the game with. So he created a beautiful goddess, Maya, just for the purpose of having fun. Once Maya existed and Brahma told her the purpose of her existence, she said, "Okay, let's play the most wonderful game, but you have to do what I tell you to do." Brahma agreed, and following Maya's instructions, he created the whole universe. Brahma created the sun and the stars, the moon and the planets. Then he created life on earth: the animals, the oceans, the atmosphere, everything.
>
> Maya said, "How beautiful is this world of illusion you created. Now I want you to create

a kind of animal that is so intelligent and aware that it can appreciate your creation." Finally Brahma created humans, and after he finished the creation, he asked Maya when the game was going to start.

"We will start right now," she said. She took Brahma and cut him into thousands of teeny, tiny pieces. She put a piece inside every human and said, "Now the game begins! I am going to make you forget what you are, and you are going to try to find yourself!" Maya created the Dream, and still, even today, Brahma is trying to remember who he is. Brahma is there inside you, and Maya is stopping you from remembering what you are."

To deny your own divinity is to deny the very thing that makes up our true essence—who we truly are. I'm not talking about this body and brain. I'm talking about the spirit that connects our bodies and minds to the eternal *Source*. Nature lives in perpetual awareness of its divinity. The elements, water, air, light, rocks, and plants don't have brains and egos to get in the way and cause them to doubt. They just exist in harmony with everything else, oblivious to mental pain. Likewise, it is in our nature to live the same way.

To consider God as something outside ourselves is to accept separation. To think that God dwells within us also implies separation as two distinct entities. Instead, consider that there is no separation at all, only a lack of awareness of your true self. As we quiet our thoughts and tame our minds, we gain a clearer picture and a greater awareness of what is real and true. We recognize our divinity, and the divinity of everyone and everything around us. You are God! You are *Love*! You are the *Source*!

It is all too easy to ascribe the mystical and miraculous to the whim of a deity. It is easy to attempt to understand the unexplained and unknown by assigning those things to a god or gods. Humanity has done this throughout its entire history. Once, the rising and setting of the sun and moon were thought to be gods chasing each other around the sky. Earthquakes and volcanoes were supposed to be the wrath of a god or gods. Even the weather was attributed to some mood of the deities. We know differently now. We know that the earth spins on its axis as it orbits the sun, giving us night and day and seasons. We know that the moon orbits the earth, and its cycle gives us moon phases that light up the night. We know that earthquakes and volcanoes occur because the earth's surface is constantly in motion. These things are no longer mysteries that are willed by some outside force, but a result of natural energies inherent in a living universe.

I don't know about raising the dead, walking on water, turning water into wine, or multiplying food, but I do know that when the power of *Love* is flowing through us unimpeded, true miracles happen. Miracles of healing— emotional, psychic, and even physical—often occur. Your very presence and the *Love* you radiate can save someone's life and bring joy to so many people. As we progress and share this *Love*, its power spreads and pushes *Fear* away.

The truth is that everything is God, and God is everything. That includes you, and by your very nature, you are God. You are *Love*—even if you aren't yet aware of it or don't feel it. As we begin to see our divinity, accept it, and connect with it, we even start to act like it. Every moment becomes a prayer of praise and gratitude. The bliss of being spiritually awake and whole is unparalleled. The joy of freedom from egocentricity borders on ecstasy.

My friends and loved ones often say to me, "John, you never meet a stranger." That's true! I may not know about all the things you've done while you've been in your body, but I know you. I know who you are. I can see your spirit is just like mine. It's the same spirit, just expressing itself through your life as well as mine.

If what I say is true—we are all just part of the expanding nature of *Love*, and our purpose is to answer the question, "Will you love me?"—then we are all God, manifesting in everything and everyone, playing out the possibilities between yes and no.

* * *

Look all around yourself. What do you see? When you are in a crowd, do you feel smaller and less significant, or do you feel much bigger? Think of all the people, animals, plants, and elements on the planet and all the diversity. This may seem weird, but consider that there is only *one* of us. In this way, you are now reading words that you actually wrote. How can this be? I see billions of other people in the world. There are probably billions of people on other planets throughout the universe! How could there be just one of us?

That's a neat trick, isn't it? Consider this: we came from eternity. Eternity has no dimension, no space, and no time. Breaking the barrier between eternity and existence allows us to enter the universe in infinite forms, an infinite number of times, and at any time. That means we can appear whenever, wherever, and in as many forms as there are. The form that we take gives us the illusion of time. The form we take becomes individual, and we interact with ourselves. In a parable, Jesus said, " 'Most certainly I tell you because you did it to one of the least of these my siblings, you did it to me' " (Matthew 24:40).

All of the energy in the universe existed at once. Energy can't be created, and it can't be destroyed, only transferred or transformed. Energy can become matter or light. Energy can be stored, consumed, and converted. The same energy that existed when the Earth was just dust floating in space billions of years ago is still around us now. We are the same energy. If God/*Love*/the *Source* is that energy, then it experiences the universe through every form it takes. For something that can't be created or destroyed, time is meaningless.

The main takeaway is that we are one. We are so much more than our perception of self or the universe. We belong in this place because this place *is* us. It's easy to imagine a supreme being because we feel limited as humans. We look at our weaknesses and failings and say things like "Nobody's perfect" to convince ourselves we are not who we really are. But if we can't do the things we think a god ought to be able to do, how could we possibly be God? We often have an idea of what kind of power and magic a god—or the God—should be able to wield. But being God doesn't mean causing floods, speaking from burning bushes, walking on water, or raising the dead. Being God isn't magical; it's mystical. We are all God (or gods), whether we acknowledge it or not. Recognizing our godhood, however, is acknowledging our connection to the universe and everything in it.

When the universe came into being, it did so with only one rule: nothing could be added, and nothing could be taken away. Everything else was fair game. Because of that, there will always be balance. Right now, you and I are in the particular form of a human person. The miracle is that we get to contemplate this existence and this form. We have minds to think of these things and explore a universe of ideas. We can create whole worlds or other universes in our dreams and imaginations.

But there is a price for that intellectual ability, because we have forgotten who we are. When we remember, though, we can connect our minds to the purest form of that energy: *Love*. That is incredibly powerful. More and more, as we wake up and remember who we are, the world changes, even just a little bit at a time. If enough people were awake and in tune with the vibration of *Love*, it would be heaven on earth.

The God in the Mirror

Have you ever looked up at the stars or felt the sun on your face and wondered, *Where do I fit in this universe?* Are you happy and content all of the time? Do you know who and what you are? Why did you choose this book? How did you feel when it called out to you, or why did someone recommend it to you?

There are forces in our universe that are often hard to understand or explain. Beyond what we can know with our senses, there is Knowledge that exists within the very framework of all creation.

When I began my spiritual journey in earnest, I picked up many books on Faith, self-actualization, spiritual freedom, inner peace and happiness, meditation—so many different spiritual teachers with many different ideas. I looked for the common thread in modern spiritual thought, New Age spirituality, and religious texts.

What I discovered is that the common thread is one word: *Love.* That wasn't too hard to grasp, but I didn't know where to begin. All these words bounced off the hardened shell around my heart. I dwelt in a house of pain, regret, and remorse, yearning for escape. My thoughts were often a jumble, regretting my past and hoping for so much better in my future. My now was a mess of desperation and impatience.

I began this journey during the worst period in my

life. I was lost and lonely and in the most excruciating emotional pain. I knew well enough that I was headed for a fall, teetering on the edge of hope and hopelessness. I was suicidal—not because I didn't want to live, so much as I just wanted the pain to end.

Then I picked up a book (now one of my essentials) called *The Four Agreements* by Don Miguel Ruiz. I had just begun to read it when the bottom (which I had thought was my rock bottom) fell out from underneath me. The only thing that spared me was the intense feeling that as far as my whole life was concerned, I'd been doing it wrong, and there was a better way; I just hadn't figured it out yet.

Splayed out at the bottom of the deepest well of despair—a low I could never have imagined—I was given a gift that I did not deserve: I found God, hiding in the last place I would have ever looked.

Throughout my years of practice and study prior to my spiritual awakening, I was always looking for God on the outside. I was trying to figure out how to behave just right so that I could feel accepted and loved by God. I was trying to do all the right things. I was trying to figure out what I needed to do to have the Holy Spirit come to dwell within me. I thought I'd done all the prescribed things, but I never felt any better. And I never felt authentic.

At a point in my life where I'd lost everything and had little hope for the future, my mind strangely quieted. I had a weird and wonderful experience with a glimpse of eternity, which has already begun to alter my mind and how I think.

But it was an epiphany that brought it all together. All those years of questing and questioning, all the fruitless searches for a God I could not understand or love... Then, not long after my experience with eternity—a couple of weeks or so—I met God face-to-face. I'd been hearing people say that the only way I was alive was because God willed it so. I don't think I believed that, but I honestly gave it some thought. One day while I was shaving, as I stared into the water and stubble-speckled foam in the sink, I had a very clear thought: *Where are you, God?* Then I looked back into the mirror...

"Oh," I said out loud, "there you are."

This wasn't a "religious experience"—far from it. As I stood there staring into the soul of that reflection, I finally realized the truth. Everything I thought I knew, everything I tried to believe was nothing more than stories that tried to explain something in a way that made no sense to me.

It wasn't that God was in me; it was the realization that God *is* me, and I am God. We all are. Everything is. Everything is made of pure energy and light. At the atomic and subatomic levels, we are indistinguishable from a rock, river, tree, bird, or star. Everything vibrates with the truth of the universe.

I finally had the spiritual awakening I'd longed for when I quit looking for it. It would be easy to say that I had been treated to a series of miracles in rapid succession, but I'd rather not. I thought so at the time, but the idea of some sort of divine intervention rubbed me the wrong way. I don't buy it. That's not to say that miracles don't happen;

they do. Just not in the way that seems to be so commonly put forth in religion and mythology.

I have come to know that the universe was created because the eternal force I call *Love* needed it to grow. *Love*, in its simplest form, is intent. When I use the word *Love* (with a capital *L*), I refer to the energetic force that exists as eternity. It has no personality and no form, and it isn't conscious. It is a paradox, because it is nothing and everything. It is the only thing that can be temporal and eternal, and it is both.

I use the word *Love* because it has an ideal attached to it. I call it *Love* because when we tap into that energy and let it flow through us, it evokes feelings and emotions associated with what we call love. When we speak of love, we speak of an emotional and visceral feeling when we say we "love" something or someone. It is also quite common for other spiritual teachers, guides, and texts to refer to this force, this energy with that exact term. Above all else, I could think of no better single word that describes it.

I use the words *Love* and *God* interchangeably. It may be confusing at times, but it generally works well in specific contexts—especially when comparing and contrasting religion, spirituality, and enlightenment. But when I say "God," I mean "*Love*," and when I say "*Love*," I mean "God." For me, they represent the same thing.

Over the years, my habits of religion and doctrine have slipped away. My first attempt at writing this book was rife with Christian religious references—not just Bible verses, but certain theological ideas, too. I wouldn't say that those ideas diminished my spirituality. I was intimately familiar with those ideas, and they were useful while I was building and developing my understanding of who I am and my place in the universe.

My ideas and thoughts are constantly in motion and ever-changing. Today, I believe that when the universe was created out of necessity, the pure force and intent of *Love* filled every atom, particle, and empty space with itself. I believe this, too, was out of necessity. Later, I will explain how I think everything came into being; suffice to say that creation happened because the nature of *Love* is to expand and grow. That is the purpose of everything and for everyone.

I believe that this force has many manifestations, and one of those is a kind of energy I call spirit. The spirit is the vehicle through which all creation communicates with itself—with *Love*. Again, ALL things are *Love*. Everything is made of *Love*, and ALL things ARE *Love*.

I believe that the purpose of this universe is to have the chance to freely accept the invitation to return to the *Source* (another word I use for *Love* and God). The nature of love is that it must be free. It must be given freely, and it must be accepted willingly. We are here to make a choice: to love *Love* back, or not.

I believe that human beings are specially equipped to tap into the *Source*, but we are equally handicapped. We are imbued with a mind capable of self-awareness through some trick of evolution. We are capable of emotion and abstract thought. Everything else we can observe lives in a constant state of grace, existing as it should in pure love. But humans got so clever that we messed it all up, complicated it, and abandoned existing in heaven to live in the nightmare of hell.

I believe that there will be a point in time when all of creation has finished considering the option and accepts the invitation, and then this universe will snap out of existence as surely as it began. The question now is "What do we do in the meantime?"

It is my experience that God is not an intercessor by Himself. Intercession and miracles do occur, but those mystical things happen due to the intent of *Love* and the purpose of the universe. These things do not happen because some benevolent entity chooses to show favor. That would be the antithesis of pure, unconditional *Love*.

A Path

The path to spiritual peace, happiness, and enlightenment is not the only path to fulfillment. Many people are content just to be and have no conscious connection to the *Source*. They are content to roll along with life's ups and downs, oblivious to the magnificence of eternal *Love*. They live, love, laugh, cry, and cuss—and that's good enough.

Then there are the *Seekers*. There are seekers of truth, seekers of wisdom, seekers of justice. Some seek to answer questions like "Why am I here?" Some seek treasure, some seek comfort; there are all kinds of ways to look for something lost or something new.

If you are reading this book, you are likely seeking something that will improve your conscious contact with God. Because we are made up of *Love*, it touches something in our minds and activates our spirit. There is an ever-present longing for most of us to commune with the *Source*. This exists in everything and everyone by degrees. The yearning is greater in some and lesser in others.

If the universe was created so that *Love* can grow and then the "new" part of *Love* can answer the question, "Will you love me?", then our purpose is to make that decision. We were created by the expansion of the *Source* with the single purpose of answering that question. For us to be able to answer that question, a moment in time had to be created, but a moment cannot exist in eternity. This moment has manifested an entire universe full of matter and energy, galaxies, stars, planets, and animals—and you.

You are light, and you are love. If you think you don't know the way to the *Source*, I am happy to tell you that yes, you do know *The Way*. You do not have to travel far—or at all. God is, and God is right where you are. If you'd like to see the face of God, grab a mirror, look at the people around you, or look outside.

What I'm saying is that you are already connected to the *Source*, because you are the *Source*! If you don't know or aren't sure about that, all you need is to awaken your spirit and awareness. Chances are that you have some sense of this already. Telling you that you are God may frighten or excite you. Or you may already be aware of this and seek a broader path or a more vital awareness.

I call the path I'm on *The Way*. It's a phrase I picked up from the New Testament; it's what the early Christian movement was called. Jesus said that He was "the way, the truth, and the life" (John 14:6), and when I began my journey, I was still heavily invested in Christian doctrine. The way I walk my path is still heavily influenced by the Bible, just not dogmatically or doctrinally. Instead, my beliefs and practices amalgamate many teachings and spiritual texts. I've taken all the bits that resonate with me and stitched them into a warm and comfortable quilt that I am happy to share with anyone who asks.

We are like elastic tendrils spun out from the center of a wheel. The *Source* (also called the One, *Love*, or God) is the hub. We were flung out and sent on a mission at the beginning of creation. The task is to accept the love of the *Source*, remember who and what we are, and answer the question, "Will you love me?" This is a metaphor, of course, but I think it illustrates the relationship we have with *Love* and the energy that is the source of everything that exists.

In geometry, there is an infinite number of rays extending outward from the center of a circle, like the spokes of a wheel. Each spoke is a straight line, but a winding path can be taken instead. Each of us has our path, though we often join with others in parallel. The paths we take toward the *Source* may look almost identical to paths others have followed. Spiritual teachers and guides may show us the shortcuts they've found, or the beauty to be seen when taking the long way.

It is often said that it isn't the destination that matters, but the journey. I agree with this because there is a fundamental flaw with my spoke-and-wheel analogy: it implies that the journey leads to somewhere, rather than to something. "Somewhere" is everywhere; "something" is the awareness of who you are. Along the path, we learn how to push away the mental image of ourselves (as self) and remove the blockages that have prevented us from realizing our ability to be conduits of *Love*. When we allow the energy of our true being to flow through and radiate from us, our awareness becomes clear.

I don't believe reaching the destination is something I'm supposed to achieve in this lifetime. It is the journey that is my purpose. I firmly believe that if I were to attain full enlightenment, neither my mind nor my body would be able to survive the experience, simply because the spirit

I carry would have no further need for the vessel it is in.

I do not believe it matters to God whether we set out on a path to achieve spiritual awareness or not. There is no real separation. Separation is an illusion created so that we can understand the fullness and freedom of *Love* itself.

Being spiritually awake or enlightened gives us the ability to appreciate the beauty of this creation in all its splendor and glory. We are perfectly free to experience this reality miserably, blissfully, or any way in between. The gift of life was never intended to be terrible or hellacious; it was meant to be enjoyed ecstatically. How this nightmare happened is a result of forgetfulness. But if we were not allowed to make mistakes, we wouldn't be free, and there would be no point at all to the universe. Instead, creation was given a chance to seek experiences freely. Somewhere along the way, a little at a time—long before the human species was born—we forgot that none of this is real.

The choice still exists. We can choose to awaken and realize that we were meant to play and have fun in this wondrous universe. We can open our eyes and understand that suffering is meaningless and quite absurd. The world believes in suffering because so much of it has forgotten how to be *Love*. That's okay if that's how you want to play. Personally, I prefer the joy of being *Love*. Honestly, pain and drama are too much work. Being awake is effortless because it is the natural state of all Being.

On the other hand, waking up is the hard part. If we've been trained to accept the world's illusion as reality and truth, and if we have been asleep all our lives just like countless generations before us, then denying the illusion is going to take some training and work. Accepting that the world is generally awful, with a few bright spots speckled about, is our tradition as a species. We accept that there is suffering, war, famine, poverty, and illness. We tend to respond by burying our heads in our tiny bubbles. We live in a world of judgment and indifference without a second thought. We mill around looking for some enjoyment, some happiness that will shut out the cold callousness of the world "out there."

If this picture seems bleak and depressing, then understand that it isn't real. Oh, but it feels very real! We lose people we love to violence. We often suffer needlessly. We feel joy and pain, hope and hopelessness.

When I first contemplated stepping out on a journey to find peace, I was very cynical. In those early days, I was not at all convinced that any amount of meditation, prayer, or even enlightenment could wipe away the insanity right outside my door. How was love supposed to fix all that mess, I wondered?

Well, that's not exactly how this illusion works. I will say with absolute certainty that if more than half of the humans on this planet woke up—even just a little bit— there would be an end to suffering on this planet. There would be no more war. Famine would not exist. No one would be homeless. Everyone would have all that they need and more than they could want.

I don't know how long it will take, but I know

that every spirit in creation will eventually wake up. Will humanity achieve this before the species goes extinct? That I do not know—and I honestly do not care. It doesn't matter.

To be filled and flowing with *Love* is to be fearless. From that perspective, the world looks quite silly in its suffering. But it is hard not to remember what it's like to suffer or have empathy for those who do. I am not suggesting that I don't care about the suffering of others; I do, and I want to do something about it. I want you to do the same. And I want you to share that with others, who will also do the same—on and on, until the moment that we no longer need this universe, and we can be whole again and simply exist.

With awareness, you see that all that suffering makes no difference and that none of creation will remember it when this purpose is fulfilled. Alive or dead, awake or asleep, joyful or sorrowful—it's meaningless within the context of what we truly are. What makes a difference is how you want to spend the time you have to experience a life (or possibly many lives) outside of eternity. I have found that being stuck in a nightmare of senseless and useless suffering is no fun at all. I find it takes more work and energy to keep the illusion propped up—mainly because all energy comes from *Love*, and a world living in *Fear* is a world that is pushing *Love* away and using up what little energy and power are left. The illusion can't sustain itself—although it seems like it can, because our time as individual humans is so short.

The point, then, is that if you are ready to surrender a senseless illusion filled with pain for the waking reality of perfect *Love*—and to experience authentic, lasting joy—then strike out on a path. Experiment and find whatever resonates with you. Accept that you can change your mind any time you like. You can believe something today and believe something else tomorrow. You are not bound by anything except your own willingness.

I truly need you to be awake, and I need you to awaken others—if for no other reason than the possibility that a life without fear and pain exists and can be achieved in this lifetime. If you accept even a little bit of what I am saying as true, you may understand that when I say, "I need," I mean, "God needs." We need everyone to wake up so that we can all go home.

Chapter Seventeen: *Life After Death*

"There is no Death! What seems so is transition;
This life of mortal breath Is but a suburb of the life elysian,
Whose portal we call Death."

— *Henry Wadsworth Longfellow*

There Is No Death

I am often asked if I believe in life after death. I say, "No, because I don't believe in death." Henry Wadsworth Longfellow wrote that there is no death, only transition. He said that our mortal life is just one stage of life in a much bigger journey—or, as he put it, this part of living is just a suburb of heaven.

At the time of this writing, my body is still alive, and I am (for the most part, at least) of sound mind. I have experienced ego death and spiritual death, and I have had transcendent experiences, too; but I cannot relate those to whatever might happen when the physical body perishes. I do have an idea that I'm pretty fond of: whatever you believe will happen is what, for you, will happen—at least until all the energy of the conscious mind has been reabsorbed into the universe.

Based on my personal experience of eternity itself, I can do no better than assume what lies ahead for any of us. I honestly don't know—and that mystery excites me. I have guesses and fantasies, but nothing at all I'd call knowledge.

Even in connecting to the collective unconscious, I have no answer. I know that a nanosecond and a thousand years are the same for eternity. During the transfer of energies from the death of a body until all the energy has dissipated, I do not doubt that consciousness could experience eternity or the passage of time.

There are many accounts of near-death experiences where the person was brought back to life, and there are many similarities between them. Some describe an experience of an empty, painless eternity without time or space—just as I experienced—and some describe a bright white light, with loved ones previously departed and/or an avatar like Jesus or Buddha to welcome them to the next life. Others still have said that whoever met them in the light told them it wasn't time, and they had to return. While there are indeed exceptions, it seems the most common thread is quiet peace.

Whatever I say here is only speculation and beliefs that are subject to change. However, the longest-held view I've had is what I believe at this moment. The conscious mind needs a brain to function. Our emotions are also functions of the brain. Our thoughts are functions of the brain. We know, scientifically at least, that when certain parts of the brain are damaged or removed, some or all of these brain characteristics are altered or removed. I do not know how connected the spirit (that exists in all things) is with consciousness. I don't know if personality is spiritual or physical. Does the spirit remain individual, or does it incorporate fully with the *Source*, like raindrops in the ocean?

While these are all fascinating questions, such speculation serves little purpose. We might try and come up with the most plausible idea and then act on it—hoping against hope that we'll do enough to make it to the reward. In my case, I can only focus on now. Such speculation on something that I have no assurance of pulls my attention away from my awareness and realization of the present—and from being present.

Not long after I awakened, I was still practicing Christianity. I still preached on occasion, and I tried to help people with the tenets of that religion combined with what I had become aware of. What became apparent to me is that (like Yoda told Luke in *Star Wars*), there is no "try"—only "do."

Jesus said that there is one primary commandment with two parts:

> [34]But the Pharisees, when they heard that he had silenced the Sadducees, gathered themselves together. [35]One of them, a lawyer, asked him a question, testing him. [36]"Teacher, which is the greatest commandment in the law?"

> [37]Jesus said to him, "You shall love the Lord your God with all your heart, with all your soul, and with all your mind." [38]This is the first and great commandment. [39]A second likewise is this, "You shall love your neighbor as yourself."

⁴⁰The whole law and the prophets depend on these two commandments (Matthew 22: 34-40, World English Bible translation).

I realized that when we connect to the *Source*—to *Love* itself—there is a transformation that occurs naturally. I'd been asked so many times, "What about sin? How can I stop sinning?" The answer was already before them. The behaviors that many religions consider "sinful" are usually byproducts of *Fear* and acting out the emotions that come with *Fear* (the lack of *Love*). What I noticed was that when we practice connecting to *Love*, our behavior shifts, and we are much more available for the benefit of others. And why wouldn't we be? To be connected to that Spirit of *Love* is to love others just as ourselves, and we know that they are us, just as we are them.

Everything we do in this world to hurt others is a result of the lack of *Love*—of the *Fear*—that creates the emptiness in us. But when we are flowing with the abundance of *Love*, we are not empty or wounded. We are whole and present. We adopt the true nature of *Love*, which is to expand, so that is what comes out of us.

Jesus said, "If a person loves me, they will keep my word. My Father will love them, and we will come to them, and make our home with them" (John 14:23). Within this biblical context, there is only one thing that anyone must actively do: love. From there, everything else falls into place naturally.

So then, if the Bible's vision of an afterlife is correct, at least I know I've got the right recipe for success. Besides that, we have nothing to lose and everything to gain by being in love with *Love*.

Not having a definitive answer to that age-old question, "Where do we go after this?" doesn't cause me any concern. Hell is a man-made concept. I refuse to accept the notion of a benevolent creator who would allow any of its creation to fall into eternal suffering, whether by choice or by force. I refuse to believe that refusing to believe is cause for such punishment, too. I have no judgment for or against anyone who chooses to believe that; it's their business. I'm only saying what I am to convey this: I do not fear death. I fear wasting this life.

"It is not death that a [person] should fear, but [they] should fear never beginning to live."

— Marcus Aurelius

Bibliography

Conway, John, C M Kosemen, Darren Naish, and Scott Hartman. 2013. *All Yesterdays: Unique and Speculative Views of Dinosaurs and Other Prehistoric Animals*. S.L. Irregular Books.

DiSalvo, David. n.d. "How Alan Turing Helped Win WWII and Was Thanked with Criminal Prosecution for Being Gay." Forbes. Accessed May 27, 2022. https://www.forbes.com/sites/daviddisalvo/2012/05/27/how-alan-turing-helped-win-wwii-and-was-thanked-with-criminal-prosecution-for-being-gay.

Jung, C G, Herbert Read, Michael Fordham, Gerhard Adler, and R F C Hull. 1966. The Collected Works of C. G. Jung. Princeton, N.J.: Princeton University Press.

Ruiz, M. (1997). The Four Agreements: A Practical Guide to Personal Freedom. Amber-Allen Publ.

Ruiz, M., & Mills, J. (1999). The Mastery of Love: A Practical Guide to the Art of Relationship. Amber-Allen Pub.

Tolle, E. (2016). A New Earth: Awakening to Your Life's Purpose (10th Anniversary Edition). Penguin Books.

(2001). Alcoholics Anonymous (Fourth Edition). Alcoholics Anonymous World Services.